(contin

"Once again, Jesse Saperstein lights the way for those living with Asperger's syndrome. *Getting a Life with Asperger's* is a priceless example for those living with Asperger's, their families, and to any of us who want to claim a bigger, fuller, and more complete life. This book and his perspective could change people's lives."

—Charles Perez, former ABC anchor, reporter and talk show host

"An invaluable, insightful, genially pragmatic, and deeply touching road map for all those with Asperger's syndrome . . . and all those with someone in their life so challenged."

—Rupert Holmes, multiple Tony Award–winning composer and author

"It is reassuring to know that my young grandson, diagnosed as being on the autism spectrum, now has an opportunity to read a book that may guide him into adulthood. Jesse Saperstein gives insight into the challenges he faced growing up with Asperger's, while offering ways to overcome these challenges. His profound words of wisdom can teach all of us how to live a successful life in the face of adversity."

—Carol DiPaolo, AIDS activist and pioneer

"*Getting a Life with Asperger's* shows readers exactly how to do just that through Jesse Saperstein's candid and exquisitely composed narrative that's stuffed full of wisdom and wit. It's the perfect second act (and let's hope not the last) to *Atypical*, his autobiography on life with Asperger's syndrome."

—Liane Holliday Willey, EdD, author of *Pretending to be Normal* and *Safety Skills for Asperger Women*

"Jesse Saperstein is an intelligent, brave new voice in the autism community. I am always wiser and happier after hearing him. He has helped me to more fully realize the untapped potential of those with autism spectrum disorders."

—Lois Rosenwald, founder and executive director of Autism Services and Resources, Connecticut

"Jesse Saperstein has written a wonderful book. It is clear, helpful, and without adornment. I cannot think of a better resource for people on the autism spectrum or for their families and friends."

—Henry David Abraham, MD, Distinguished Life Fellow of the American Psychiatric Association, co-recipient of the 1985 Nobel Peace Prize and author of *The No-Nonsense Guide to Drugs and Alcohol*

"Jesse is quite simply a teacher. With his second book he takes us on a journey through the transition into adulthood that can teach not only autistic young adults but contains wisdom that can benefit neurotypical adolescents and young adults as well. Jesse invites the reader to learn from his mistakes with humor, honesty, and concrete advice as he (and they) tries to figure out this 'thing called life.'"

—Kristie Koenig, Associate Professor and Chair, NYU Department of Occupational Therapy

"In *Getting a Life with Asperger's*, Jesse Saperstein shares his experiences, wit, and wisdom about a road traveled by few but experienced by many. It reminds us that life's hurdles affect each of us differently, but they can be overcome with effort, understanding, and humor. This book should be on the bookshelf of anyone with Asperger's syndrome, their parents, teachers, friends, neighbors, and coworkers."

—Michael D. Powers, PsyD, director of The Center for Children with Special Needs, Glastonbury Connecticut, and the Yale Child Study Center

"This book is a marvelous collection of practical wisdom from a peer who acquired it the hard way: living and learning. As a sixty-five-year-old reader, I can't imagine anyone in our Asperger's syndrome community who would not benefit from reading this!"

—Jerry Newport, Asperger's adult and coauthor of three bestselling books on Asperger's syndrome

"Jesse Saperstein is a trailblazer in the world of autism—both literally and figuratively. He is forging a new path for all individuals on the autism spectrum and changing the way we perceive ASD, all while helping us look at these individuals' abilities instead of disabilities. Thank you, Jesse, for being the catalyst that opened my eyes to my son's potential."

—Nancy Alspaugh-Jackson, autism advocate, Emmy Award–winning producer, author, and mother of son with autism

GETTING A LIFE

A LIFE

WITH ASPERGER'S

∎ ∎ ∎

Lessons Learned on the
Bumpy Road to Adulthood

JESSE A. SAPERSTEIN

A Perigee Book

A PERIGEE BOOK
Published by the Penguin Group
Penguin Group (USA) LLC
375 Hudson Street, New York, New York 10014

USA • Canada • UK • Ireland • Australia • New Zealand • India • South Africa • China

penguin.com

A Penguin Random House Company

Library of Congress Cataloging-in-Publication Data

Saperstein, Jesse A.
Getting a life with Asperger's : lessons learned on the bumpy road to adulthood / Jesse A. Saperstein.
pages cm
A Perigee book.
ISBN 978-0-399-16668-6 (paperback)
1. Saperstein, Jesse A.—Mental health.   2. Asperger's syndrome—Patients—United States—
Biography.   3. Asperger's syndrome—Patients—Life skills guides.   I. Title.
RC553.A88S275 2014
616.85'88320092—dc23
[B]
2014011613

First edition: August 2014

PRINTED IN THE UNITED STATES OF AMERICA

10   9   8   7   6   5   4   3   2   1

To my sister, Dena.

Thank you for always looking out for me as I continue my journey.

CONTENTS

INTRODUCTION

Our experience as parents of a child with autism has made us better parents and better people. Eric has taught us patience and to accept difference. He has a knack for doing typical things in atypical ways. It seems like he is telling us, "Have patience. My way may take longer, but it will get the job done!" May that always serve him well. Jason, Eric's older brother, reminds us, "Hey, Eric may use his fork backwards, but he still gets the food into his mouth!" Jason is a fantastic role model and has a unique connection and dedication to Eric that we hope lasts their lifetime. If you watch and listen, then your child with autism will teach you. We hope Eric will attend college. He has talked about wanting to be a teacher one day. We are grateful for all we learn from Eric on a daily basis.

Eric is now seven years old. He is a true free spirit. He is the most happy-go-lucky person you will ever meet. You want to be him. If society did not apply pressure to march in the typical parade of life, then Eric would float, fly, and flutter as the very best colorful butterfly he could be!

What we do know is that he has made tremendous progress and the future looks bright. At first, there were many concerns about his ability to function in the world. Would he talk, could he connect, will he be happy? We still worry about those things, but now we are excited to see what kind of person he will become in adulthood.

—Stacey and Brian Orzell

Many of my childhood memories are intertwined with trauma due to my inappropriate, often bizarre, behavior. Ninety percent of my actions were motivated by the justification of "I just wanted to see what would happen." My nickname at summer camp was "Jesse the Troublemaker." One afternoon, the bus transported a group of six-year-olds and me to a lake infested with turtles and shimmering sunfish. I darted to the exit at the back of my bus with the colorful emergency insignia and wondered what would happen if I pushed the handle in a counterclockwise direction. Like the man wielding a sledgehammer to flaunt his strength at a cheap carnival, I wanted to show off and attract an audience. A siren blared as a frantic counselor pushed the lever back to its upright position. I cried my eyes out as she grabbed my wrist.

"What are you doing? Don't you know you could have fallen out and been left behind?!"

This behavior erupted like a case of hives and then receded without a trace. I loved "making things happen" and relished the power to manipulate adults like marionettes with my antics. Adults were also in the dark as to why I was so different and recklessly exacerbated my social troubles by finding creative ways to seize negative attention.

Think back to your own antics and laugh once in a while

because it is healthier than dwelling on the shame. What did you do for negative attention either on purpose or because you did not know better? A woman recently told me about her nephew who was disciplined after knocking down a teacher the day he chose to walk sideways through the entire school like a crab. Only the Asperger's mind could come up with such brilliance mixed with pointless mayhem. Unfortunately, it often takes years for brilliance to become the dominant factor. A cache of scathing criticism has damaged some of us into not giving ourselves the freedom to be unique and embrace the fundamental advantages of being on the autism spectrum.

Until I was diagnosed with autism at the age of fourteen, my bad behavior was chalked up to immaturity. All that changed when I received the diagnosis. Suddenly, the psychiatrist who had always reminded me of that villain from *Raiders of the Lost Ark* gave me the perfect explanation and a carte blanche for all kinds of misbehavior when he said, "Jesse, I think I know what is going on with you. You have something called Asperger's, which is the mildest form of autism." After that conversation in the psychiatrist's office, I viewed high-functioning autism as a two-year-old brother still in the babbling, parrot stage of childhood development. He was the perfect scapegoat as someone too innocent to get into trouble and not verbal enough to defend himself against false accusations. A child will do just about anything to avoid consequences and responsibility. Therefore, this psychiatrist gave me the perfect gift that allowed me to "get away with murder" for the rest of my youth.

As I got older, transitioning into my teen years and twenties, I came to see that inappropriate behavior was no longer something I could easily blame on Asperger's syndrome. Others did not dismiss my comments or actions as simply quirky, cute, or different. Now they were creepy, troubling, and not acceptable.

Welcome to the Real World

When I was a kid, the worst that often happened as a result of inappropriateness was earning a detention or scolding from an adult. Now consequences seem to have a nuclear half-life and bouncing back is a long-term process. All of a sudden, the inappropriate pursuit of women or having a meltdown at a job site were serious actions followed by brutal consequences. These are lessons I learned the hard way.

The process of becoming an adult isn't easy for anyone, whether they are on the spectrum or not. It's a slow shift in attitudes and priorities, which often comes with a steep learning curve as we try to understand what others expect of us and what we want for ourselves.

Everyone is different, but if you happen to be on the spectrum, it is highly possible that you are also trying to break away from youthful behavioral patterns that are no longer serving you well. On bad days, the acrid memories bounce around my head of those times when I was punished due to an inability to understand boundaries. We have the proclivity to blurt out comments without considering the comfort zones of others. Perhaps it wasn't entirely our fault, or perhaps it was. The process of letting go is a hobbling marathon, and the tendency to dwell is often at the surface. These feelings remain stagnant like murky groundwater in a Florida marshland, and it does not take much for these emotions to rise to the surface as though an underground volcano has become active.

Each of us deals with our demons in a different way. Some choose therapy or explosive tantrums, even though a temper is the only thing you cannot get rid of by losing it. Others are dependent on video games to experience the thrill of virtual victory and subsisting on the diet of routine, family support, or disability payments. Some have jobs that are occasionally interrupted by misunderstandings, but there is a niche that has been carved. Others are veterans of job terminations due to a mixture of poor luck and repeating the same behavioral patterns responsible for such devastation.

Are you the beautiful, but spacey, woman whose exotic features became a double-edged sword? How could someone so talented and intelligent have such trouble showing up to places on time or carrying on a conversation? This book may not profile your struggles as much as it should because it is written from the point of view and experiences of an adult male. But the mildness of your differences may have prevented you from obtaining the services that could have shaved off some of your suffering. Hopefully you also see your beauty and talent that is reflected in such celebrities as Daryl Hannah and Susan Boyle, who recently opened up to the public about their own diagnosis.

Or are you like me—also struggling to build your adult life after a rough start? Were there fewer resources? Do you continue to make strides but still harbor bitterness for what does not exist? If you are lucky, any bitterness is serving as an accelerant toward earning the life you are meant to enjoy. And you could be the overcompensating Aspie who is holding things together with a stable life or maybe even a successful career and family. You have to work harder to say the right things and the labored self-control is manifested as being uptight . . . trying too hard. You are determined to hold on to what you have built and fear it may disappear like most entities that shimmer for a while. Or perhaps you are the quintessential cool uncle, the perfect babysitter, because you are happy to get down on the floor to play with toys.

I think there is "aspie" in all of us.

—Michael Buchanan, author of *The Fat Boy Chronicles*

We Are Not Alone

In reality, Asperger's syndrome is all around us in the guise of coded messages that rise like illuminated, 3-D digits in *A Beautiful Mind*. There are the obvious "closeted" cases in the form of Sheldon Cooper on *The Big Bang Theory* or Abed Nadir on *Community*, but sometimes I wonder whether SpongeBob SquarePants is also a carrier of our uniqueness for the following reasons:

- He has the most benevolent intentions of any fictionalized entity but constantly lands in trouble while inadvertently endangering lives.

- SpongeBob is oblivious to personal boundaries and is even guilty of activities that are illegal in the real world such as entering his neighbor Squidward's house without permission to surprise him in the middle of the night.

- His routine is set in stone with an entire wardrobe consisting of the same outfit every day of the week.

- The animated and porous marine organism is vulnerable to being taken advantage of and sets his standards lower than he deserves by working at the same underpaid job with a tyrannical, penny-pinching boss.

- SpongeBob is obsessed with catching jellyfish and worshipping two has-been, geriatric superheroes named

Mermaid Man and Barnacle Boy. These special interests often take the place of more adult pursuits such as romance.

- He is honest to a fault and incapable of lying.

The qualities we are sharply berated for actually exist in plenty of others who are somehow more respected and lionized in our popular culture. But their conduct is much worse and somehow they receive more of a break than us. Or they seem to bounce back sooner. It is funny and frightening at the same time in a Lewis Carroll–like universe of nonsense. Have you ever witnessed a celebrity behaving badly and thought to yourself, "Even with my case of Asperger's syndrome, I would never do that!"

I wrote this book to help ease the transition to adulthood with Asperger's. Growing up is not a smooth process, but it also offers us freedom and a chance to create the life we truly desire. I am not a therapist, doctor, career counselor, relationship expert, lawyer, or other licensed professional. However, I am living with Asperger's and doing the best I can just like so many of you. As you read further, I am hoping you will find new strategies to do the following:

- Work for the life you deserve.

- Advocate for yourself, and also forgive yourself when missteps occur. Educate others in the hopes that some will also have compassion for your past blunders.

- Strive for full, meaningful employment to the best of your ability. We have a disability, but are not disabled. Asperger's should never stop us from maintaining employment even if our choices are not ideal. The rate of unemployment for those on the autism spectrum is between 80 and 90 percent. We are capable of doing much better than this, especially considering so many of the qualities of those with Asperger's are perfect for the job setting.

- Know when to hold on and when to let go. This is something that you will have to learn on your own, but clarity will eventually come when vestigial baggage or rituals seem to usher more grief than positivity into your life. (And when you succeed in doing this, perhaps you can give me some tips as we navigate this path together.)

- Share what you have learned with others on the spectrum, especially the next generation. Yes, many of them have access to stronger resources and more awareness than we did in our childhoods. Nonetheless, counseling our younger peers while speaking to them without judgment or condescension should be our lifelong duty.

- Always have a goal in mind and pursue productivity, especially during times of stasis. "Idle hands are the devil's workshop." I am not talking about scheduling your life like a CEO, but trouble tends to find us when we are unfocused, as we turn to activities that are not always conducive to success.

- Work with the neurotypical population, not against them, as we all unite to reach our full potential. Regardless of what has happened in the past, we need each other in order to thrive.

We have a series of accomplishments to be proud of and deserve to show the world who we really are. We inhabit integrity and innovation, and will hold on to the right things. In some cases, we faced the same challenges as any other young adult without significant social challenges. But in other cases, our suffering seemed too draconian and some societal education would have made a dramatic difference. If you are bitter and cannot move past it, please think of your future as the first warm days of spring after the most brutal of winters. Eventually, the cracks and damage caused by its wrath will heal, and we will end the cycle by sharing what we've learned with others.

We have much to look forward to as we become architects of our own progress . . .

THE ROAD OUT OF LOSERVILLE STARTS HERE

I looked around my room in the fall of 2007 and saw nothing beyond a static museum whose appearance was barely altered from my high school years nearly a decade earlier. It was a testament to inertia and arrested maturity. To the left of my Disney figurines was a rotting corsage taped to the wall like a memento from Miss Havisham's mansion in *Great Expectations*. At one point, it was in full bloom and pinned onto the tuxedo of a young man on the cusp of leaving high school for a fresh start. But there was no fresh start in college, and like many of us with Asperger's syndrome, I waited in that room for too long as realities improved at a glacial pace. This was the first sign that I had entered the state of purgatory feared by many of us suffering from any type of social challenge. I had crossed the border into "Loserville."

The floor had become a patchwork quilt of soiled boxer shorts, and the bed was a permanent holding station for rancid socks. The only thing that sustained me during that period was a twelve-hour night-shift job at a computer manufacturing complex, where I subsisted on a cocktail of Red Bulls and deli food. This was followed by an eight-hour nap from 7:15 a.m. to the late afternoon. Happiness came in weekly spurts when the check finally arrived. Money never buys happiness, but it sure helps to create a superficial euphoria, for at least a little while.

Your stint in Loserville will possibly be exacerbated by relatives who cower behind good intentions or concern about your well-being. But their tone seems to point out your perpetual failures and, in many cases, remind themselves that their own children are doing a little better. Their advice is a variation on a TV talk show's tough love or the grandiose belief they have become autism experts overnight by Googling your condition on two nonconsecutive occasions. These obscure relations typically have their own skeletons in the closet, and a little detective work will flush them out. But most of the time, it is best to chalk up their tough talk to insecurity and move forward.

You may wake up at noon after a long night of watching syndicated sitcoms on Netflix and look down. You are twenty pounds overweight and have not held down a job in months. Facebook posts from high school acquaintances proposing to their girlfriends and/or celebrating yet another promotion are merely jabbing reminders that you are still moving like a backsliding glacier. You also would have slept longer, but the shrieking of the kitchen phone jolts you out of bed. It is another obscure relation asking about your job prospects and saying in an accusatory fashion, "Did you just wake up?!"

There are a few more signs to indicate that you are in a slump:

■ **A step backward into age-inappropriate interests and time wasters.** When life seems to be showing little mercy, it is a common defense mechanism to regress back to a more magical era. A perfect example would be when the Tom Hanks character makes an impulsive pilgrimage back to Cape Cod in the movie *Splash* after being dumped by his live-in girlfriend. Some of us hold on to gems from our childhood whether it is *Teenage Mutant Ninja Turtles* or YouTube's treasure trove of untapped nostalgia. (Just typing "Disney Promos from the 1980s" will open the floodgates for a hollow walk down Memory Lane, at least for me.) If video games are one of your passions, then addictive gameplay in the *Sims* or *World of Warcraft* realm melts away countless hours. In other words, the passion for battling with rage-filled, anthropomorphic birds on your phone has replaced real life. Your parental figures are also going backward and are now caring for an adult nine-year-old who has access to electronic sustenance without limits. Your life has become a virtual masturbatorium in the sense that it feels very good until you realize you are only playing with yourself. While there is nothing wrong with nostalgia or time wasters, in the adult world we are expected to get our nonsensical fix and return to reality. But you can't and fall deeper into an aimless lifestyle.

■ **A lack of success in romantic endeavors.** Pursuing sexual relationships has never been your strong suit, but even a broken watch is correct twice a day. There used to be occasional breaks in your romantic failures, but not lately. Or as the late Rodney Dangerfield once said, "You see vultures flying around your crotch." No action, and no prospects, for a long time running.

■ **A lack of steady employment.** The longer you are unemployed, the harder it is to get back in the game. Eventually you will come to see that it's not just autism that is holding you back, but other factors, challenges, and habits that are treatable through a variety of practices and resources. In my opinion, the most effective technique of all is allowing yourself the opportunity to fail in order to learn from your mistakes.

■ **Reviving useless relationships.** You may have a difficult time accepting that the lab partner from high school chemistry wants nothing to do with you. He is your Facebook friend and occasionally "likes" the comments you post on his Wall, but this is rarely an invitation for a full-blown friendship. The fourth-grade teacher who acted as a buoy for your self-esteem fifteen years ago has moved on to current students and priorities that require incessant attention. He or she may be gracious with the first email or phone call but grow increasingly annoyed when we push for a relationship. (The only time this may work is if the other individual is in a similar state of desperation and you cling to one another like human life preservers.) Of course, this is perceived as a personal slight and augments our despair.

■ **Being unprepared for transitions.** It is my personal opinion that we are more vulnerable toward failure and depression during periods of transition. The greatest joy in life is the adventure of experiencing new things, but it is also one of life's greatest challenges, at least for many of us on the spectrum. We are expected to let go of the old routine and the relationships that took months or even years to forge. Our last journey certainly had potholes, but it was just barely stable enough. We now must dive into a new experience where we are forced to learn everything the hard way with lingering consequences. Nobody gives us a warning and new expectations come with the territory. The years lost because of my erratic behavior have sent me on a lifelong journey to give others that fighting chance. One should aspire to become the Asperger's Catcher in the Rye who keeps our peers from making a blind run off a cliff. We should also help create a society where redemption is no longer a pipe dream and one's despair can be mercifully brief.

My time in Loserville lasted at least three years. It started immediately after I returned from the Appalachian Trail where I had just completed a hike of 2,174 miles to benefit the Joey DiPaolo AIDS Foundation. Most of my fellow hikers were not judgmental or fearful of my Asperger's because they were hiking with the same demons while running from a past sprinkled with trauma. My progress was gauged at the rate of 2.5 miles per hour, and no matter how brutal the physical agony may have been, it was possible to envision the finish line and cessation of physical suffering. Whenever I reached a hotel room or amenity-saturated town after seventy or eighty miles, the senses became unnaturally euphoric like a child's gimlet-eyed gaze on Christmas morning. Coming back to real life was not easy. The adult world held no such predictability, and there were not always rewards for fighting the good fight. Whenever mistakes were made on the trail, the next day was a clean slate polished even further by compensation from yesterday's failures.

Inappropriate behavior and meltdowns had lingering consequences within my local community, however. It would take years to undo the damage and dig myself out of "social pariah" status. Even as a somewhat public figure, I am still getting myself into occasional trouble (but that is a story for another chapter).

It is during this period of inertia and stasis that our former tormentors revisit us. Insults and bullying remarks from the past come back to mind, and we wonder whether they were simply speaking the truth. *After all, they called me a "loser," and look at me now.*

But most of the time you are not as much of a failure as you think, and everything only *seems* like a permanent fall from grace. You may be more of an inspiration than you realize. For example, a few positive things have come out of the economic crisis forcing us to embrace some values from the Great Depression. It has made heroes out of those who work for a living, taking whatever position they can find. My family always taught me to never look down on someone who maintains any form of honest employment. The worker carving hard rolls at a Subway may be doing the best he/she can to support a family. The true infrastructure of our country would implode without this system of symbiosis, and playing our part is something to be respected and valued.

If you are someone on the autism spectrum who is maintaining employment, you should never consider yourself to be a loser. If you're holding down a steady job, that's even more true. In fact, you have beaten the odds, considering that 80 to 90 percent of your peers are unemployed. It makes no difference whether you are the eccentric microbiologist who just accepted the Nobel Prize in Stockholm or the circus worker following the elephants around with a shovel. Take pride in your work and build on your success in that arena, as modest as it might seem.

Exiting Loserville

Your sad existence did not happen overnight. Escaping will not be an overnight process either. The first step is lauding ourselves for even our smallest accomplishments. This process may literally start at our fingertips. A little personal hygiene—clipping, cleaning, shaving—goes a long way, and if you are like me, you can eliminate the fear that you are going blind simply by wiping the film off your glasses.

Your goals at first should never be too lofty. Your ambition is to always be a little less pathetic than the day before. On day one it is critical to have only one goal in mind and milk out the task all day long in between spurts of *Scooby-Doo* episodes or whatever other addictive time waster floats your boat. You will spend all day long tackling your room, and the project will progress like an archaeological expedition. The first emotion will come in waves of shame for letting it degenerate for this long. As your family is hanging Christmas wreaths in mid-December, you may encounter a mildew-stained bathing suit from that final swim in early September. Each batch of filthy garments will be nuked in the washing machine like poltergeists in the *Ghostbusters* movies. Legend has it that if you put your ear up to the washing machine, you should be able to hear the pitiful wails of microorganisms as they perish in the rinse cycle.

The clean clothes will then be folded one bag at a time and put away in their respective drawers. Life would be much easier if we had a clean-as-you-go policy, but the majority of us cannot handle these standards. We have only two degrees of tidiness: clean or shamefully filthy. (Plenty of us on the autism spectrum do not regularly entertain company so there is little incentive to polish our personal space.) An actual floor will become visible, and you will be overwhelmed by sensations of accomplishment. The greatest reward is the euphoric shock value each time you open the bedroom door, and it looks like someone else's space. This will be the one time in your life when it is critical to show yourself the mercy that may or may not come from someone else. It may also help to dust off one age-inappropriate ritual from your childhood, and in my case, it was Roller Magic in Hyde Park, New York. The realities of life will eventually get too unbearable and will send you backward for just a little while. Vitality returned as I rekindled my love affair with the *Ms. Pac-Man* machine that still clung to its lone corner and squinted against the seizure-inducing lights. Ultimately, I would end up having my last three birthday parties in the complex and turned the most recent celebration into a massive autism fund-raiser for the community. You may be vilified for being "weird," but self-esteem will return when you find ways to share your eccentricities.

I encourage you to remain realistic and understand the feelings of despair are merely in a state of dormancy after any long-term orgasm of motivation. Even the most prolific and successful individuals in the world experience failures and setbacks in all aspects of life, including work, money, and relationships. And if they are good role models, they will own up to these episodes of ineptitude. Michael Jordan supposedly locked himself in his room and cried after being cut from his high school basketball team. Thomas Edison failed approximately one thousand times while trying to find the correct filaments for the incandescent lightbulb. Or take Nick Vujicic, who is an Australian motivational speaker who was born without limbs. Most of the time he maintains a positive attitude while giving more than two hundred fifty speeches a year, but there are definitely those more dismal times. As he admits in his memoir, *Unstoppable: The Incredible Power of Faith in Action*:

> *My mental paralysis left me unable to make even the most minor decisions. Normally, I fly through the day making dozens of important decisions regarding my schedule, projects, and other business. During this troubled time I couldn't decide whether to get out of bed or whether I should try to eat.*

You will also go backward in order to move forward, and it has nothing to do with Asperger's. This is a reality of becoming an adult when success is less predictable, more unattainable, less of an entitlement, and never gauged at the consistency of 2.5 miles per hour.

The strategies toward reversing behavioral patterns and attitudes that have contributed to these problems are different for each of us. But here are a few tips that have worked for me as well as a few of my peers on the autism spectrum:

■ **Make yourself useful.** The couch is not just a piece of furniture when we are struggling. It is a grasping, manipulative blob of fabric that will mold to your ass cheeks so gradually. Then it is always too late when one grows wise to its intentions. As is the case with many in our population, you may be living at home in your twenties . . . thirties . . . and a select few make it into their forties! It is crucial to continue working on the goals of employment, independent living, and romantic relationships. But while these goals are slowly coming to fruition, you can give yourself a surge of self-worth by being a dynamo of dishwashing, a sultan of snow shoveling, the grocery shopper, the landscape architect (aka weed puller), and the martyr chained to litter-box-sifting duties. These efforts will not go unnoticed or unappreciated by your family, as you continue moving in the right direction. Much of your negativity is created by feelings of worthlessness, and the psychological panacea will be to make yourself feel useful. A sufficient holding pattern will emerge until something better comes along.

■ **Find an Asperger's support group.** Your muddy predicament is too opaque to navigate by yourself, and being around like-minded individuals will shave off some of your distress. It is instructive and useful to meet a few of your peers who have been walking this road for years with varying degrees of success along the way. Besides making some new friends, these fellow travelers will serve as a think tank of strategies for your emancipation from Loserville.

You may find yourself serving as a role model to those who are in far worse shape when you thought that you were the last person worthy of admiration. There will also be group members who have escaped a similar predicament and will be able to simultaneously empathize as well as offer advice. Recreational activities such as trips to museums are often an extension of these support groups. When we are struggling, it can be a very alienating experience, and this support will reinforce that you are not alone. Most important, recovery will become a luminescent sliver on the horizon.

■ **Seek professional help.** Some of you have nursed a bitter grudge against mental health professionals, especially if you were forced into therapy as a young child. Perhaps you feel a stigma associated with therapy. A good therapist will have some knowledge of Asperger's and successfully worked with some of your peers. I have always believed a decent therapist should serve as more of a life coach, looking forward more than backward. They will work with you beyond solving your psychological strife, but also function as a sounding board and reality check while you are working to build your life aspirations.

Furthermore, the barriers preventing you from Couch Liberation may be due to a chemical imbalance that must be treated with professional intervention.

■ **Early to bed, early to rise, makes a man healthy, wealthy, and . . .** As far as irritation triggers are concerned, this phrase probably bugs me even more than "Others have it worse" and "Where was the last place you saw it?" But the times I was in the deepest trenches of my slump involved a pattern of watching television until 4:00 a.m. while making a half-assed attempt to apply for jobs during the commercials. Then I would wake up by noon and realize the day had been wasted followed by a spasm of self-disgust. The pattern repeated itself for months and was only broken by the extremes of two cell phone alarm clocks set in six increments of a half-hour apart from each ring. A good morning begins before eight o'clock and the juices of productivity flow with menial chores involving turd maintenance (aka litter-box cleaning) and dishwashing. Shift your schedule a bit earlier and see for yourself.

■ **Chart your progress.** Whether you keep a diary or journal, notes on your smartphone, or jottings on a wall calendar, keeping track of your efforts and the fruits they are bearing will help you stay the course. Think of ways to quantify your success—number of days in a row the bed was made, or number of weekends you did laundry, sent out your résumé, or reached other daily and weekly goals. Success breeds success, so make sure you're paying attention.

■ **Take a break from Facebook.** Facebook and other social media sites are truly a vortex of lost productivity. Perhaps one of these days our society will organize a boycott of Facebook. It would be one week in which people would not be allowed to post status updates about banal accomplishments involving dog walking or showering that receive inevitable "likes." The obsessive postings of status updates regarding diaper changing and parental woes involving projectile vomiting will be placed on a much needed back burner. The same standards would hold true for unrelenting "poking" and pleas to join addictive gameplay such as *Mafia Wars*. There is nothing that will consume an entire day faster than relinquishing one's soul to social media. Ignored friendship requests and moping about the photos of your high school crush's wedding will exacerbate your motivational slump. But most of us are not going to give it up cold turkey anytime soon. Perhaps Facebook can be your reward after a day of productivity. And when you succeed in making this happen, please share your secret with the rest of us who are still struggling to put this modern-day distraction in its place.

■ **Get some exercise.** Take a walk. Shoot some basketball hoops. Whatever works for you. You might find a Fitbit, Fuel-

Band, fitness app, or similar tool useful for charting progress and staying motivated.

■ **Volunteer in your community.** "When you help others . . . you're really helping yourself!" This is a line that comes from *Avenue Q*, an off-Broadway musical starring X-rated *Sesame Street*–like Muppets. But it holds true regarding the power to impact your community. It will be your salvation to have a reason to wake up before 8:00 a.m. at least four days a week. Whether it is volunteering at a soup kitchen, working with animals at a shelter, or handing out candy at a Halloween celebration for disadvantaged children . . . it is important to give something back, and introduce yourself to a community where connections are forged. Volunteering definitely has an altruistic incentive, although I would rather refer to it as "employment with a safety net." Volunteering may not involve payment (unless there is a small stipend for necessities like travel expenses), but it can be similar to having an actual job, and the supervisors will be more lenient toward mistakes. It is more practical to learn from a mistake while volunteering than when you have a real job and could very well endanger your employment. And these connections will inevitably lead to other opportunities. The greatest myth about those of us with Asperger's is that we lack empathy or are not meant to be part of the mainstream social world. Therefore, let your actions refute this myth as you make strides to show that you can be counted on to complete tasks and display incremental improvements. Most important, when it comes time to apply for a real job, you will have supporters to vouch for your potential.

We must accept that the process of building or rebuilding your life will not happen overnight. "Loserville" may stalk you even when you escape, and it is important to understand that motivation is a mental muscle that can rapidly atrophy without nearly constant stimulation. But the hard work is worth it. The rewards you create from this newfound resurgence of initiative will have more of a potent sweetness because you made the success happen yourself, the hard way.

GETTING OUT
FROM THE SHADOW
OF BULLYING

I t is interesting to look back at our earlier years and wonder, "What were they thinking?" As much as I hate to trample on a beloved classic like *Rudolph, the Red-Nosed Reindeer*, this clay-animated Yuletide gem reinforces bullying because of someone's birth defect. It also encourages adults to join in the torment. While Rudolph's heroics fill the story with magic, the message is sent that in order to earn universal acceptance, one must ascend to feats of unrealistic heroism. Mine was the last generation that did not flinch against these warped jewels of nostalgia. The solution is not to yank *Rudolph* from its annual appearance on cable, but to hope that parents explain that this is not the proper way to treat individuals who are different.

Whether you were teased, mocked, tormented, excluded,

or just on the receiving end of cold shoulders and disapproving glances, odds are strong that you experienced some form of bullying as a child. You might be tempted to think that as an adult you've put these experiences behind you, and in some ways you probably have. But the wounds of bullying can run deep. With every rejection, failed first impression, and job termination, the old pain can resurface.

Chances are good that you also grew up in an environment when bullying was accepted as a childhood rite of passage, or worse, a self-inflicted consequence of choosing to not conform. Teachers ignored your misery in hopes it would naturally fade away. There were also no anti-bullying assemblies and the schoolyard sprawled out like a Darwinian war zone. When a large group of those with Asperger's congregates, the war stories will unsuppress themselves, and a wellspring of pain, humiliation, and even bitterness comes to life. A friend at my support group once revealed that a female classmate handed her a dog bone wrapped in a festive bow as a Christmas present.

Moving Forward

One of the greatest challenges you will face in adulthood is how to move forward with a festering chamber of unresolved memories. There were times when others showed kindness and even acknowledged your potential. But such moments of mercy may have been too rare and are overshadowed by the slurs of "retard, psychopath, stalker, and weirdo." Becoming an adult should be your chance to move forward. Even if you cannot completely expel these memories, letting them hold you back will be an enormous disservice to you and those who may benefit from your passion.

When my first book was released in 2010, people started to come out of the woodwork to offer their congratulatory wishes and apologies. They have learned that bullying does not just affect victims but perpetrators as well. I was told it may be worth your energy to take a chance and contact some of your past tormenters just to ask, "Why?"

Stop Blaming Yourself

Our neurotypical peers easily found ways to justify physical/emotional abuse. My shenanigans such as spontaneously singing the national anthem and flaunting erections in math class did not help as far as decreasing bullying. On the other hand, schoolyard culture was not conducive to earning attention the positive way. I was not athletic enough to stand out for my sports achievements or academically outstanding enough to gain recognition that way either. Some of you may have engaged in similarly "strange" behaviors; I hear about them all the time from friends who work with my young peers. There was the little boy whose passion is bathroom humor and describes in vivid detail about what his excrement looks like in the toilet. Or the girl who dresses in an anime costume nearly every day. I recently performed a radio interview with my old Sunday school teacher who admitted that she could not understand how I, a fourth-grade boy who was so adorable and intelligent, could do so many ridiculous things to exacerbate my torment. Nobody knew that I was on the autism spectrum at the time, but she pleaded with my mother to put me on medication after I knocked down half the classroom books while walking around aimlessly with my eyes shut.

Regardless of why you were bullied back then, there are ways to push through the experience—to live with the scars without letting them define you or hold you back.

You Are No Longer Alone

Perhaps it was common for you to find comfort in TV characters whose quirks resembled your own. There was Samuel "Screech" Powers, who was highly intelligent, but was painfully deficient in common sense. The TV character I felt the most empathy for was Gonzo (aka the Weirdo) from the animated Jim Henson spin-off *Muppet Babies*. Gonzo did not belong anywhere with his blue fur and enormous, hook-like nose. I often felt like Gonzo in the sense that few groups understood me enough to embrace me in their flock of unified, adolescent angst. Regardless of your coping strategies back then, now that you are grown, you can take comfort in knowing there are actual people (not just fictionalized beings) who share your plight. Seek them out through support groups. Read about the effects of bullying, and realize that you are one of many, no longer the lone scapegoat in a crowd.

Seek Out Catharsis

It has a different meaning for everybody, but to me, one of the most powerful forms of catharsis—the purging of negative emotions—comes with revisiting the situation that created the poison in the first place. The person who was traumatized by the bite of a black widow spider makes the decision to visit a tarantula farm where she allows the arachnids to stalk her flesh. Like a bulldog, you may want to try exposing yourself to nuggets of pain (carefully, and with the support of trusted friends and family), especially when it comes to inspiring the next generation.

One of my long-time goals came to fruition in November 2010 when I had the chance to speak to Arlington Middle School, which I attended from 1994 to 1996. The hallways looked the same, but they were now populated by schoolchildren carrying iPhones and cell phones buzzing with Facebook status updates about their "friends" having breakfast and brushing their teeth. In my day, the coolest device that students carried to school was perhaps a CD player. While the Internet existed when I was in middle school, it was not ubiquitous, wireless, or an extension of schoolyard terror. A child could return home to their veritable haven and remain sheltered from such pain or at least decompress from some of the impact that transpired earlier in the day.

Another way to reach catharsis could be to compose a letter to your former perpetrators. This idea might be frowned upon by some who believe you must let sleeping dogs lie, but it may actually lead to a sense of closure if you dare attempt it. It is just as important to prepare yourself for a defensive response—or absolutely no response, for that matter. You could consider doing this for anyone who has caused anguish, including adult authority figures. Also consider writing the letter but not sending it, as a way to get the feelings off your chest and onto the page.

Look in the Mirror

With that said, before we condemn some of our past victimizers as villains, it is important to examine our own house. People with disabilities can be both victims and perpetrators. For all we know, you could have been the one doing the bullying yourself, and maybe it would help to make amends. The bullying could have been inadvertent considering it was not necessarily malicious but took the form of brutal honesty united with the lack of a filter mechanism. Like psychological aftershocks that involuntarily fire while giving anti-bullying speeches, I still remind myself of the time when I was eight years old, and I repeatedly slapped a nonverbal student with a seat belt on the school bus as he made grimaces of pain. Just having that power over someone else as a second grader made me feel alive. And the main reason why I did not escalate into worse forms of bullying is because of the swift reactions of those who steered me in a different direction.

Share Your Wisdom

It should be the duty of the Asperger's population to advocate for our younger peers and youths of all abilities whose self-esteem is less developed until they have nursed enough confidence to have faith in their own voices. Let them know the difference between constructive criticism and feedback that is cruel or ridiculous.

I believe the autism population could accomplish great things even if we cannot necessarily let go and forgive when recounting our own bullying experiences. We could become Deacons of the Movement. Public orators on the autism spectrum are pathetically few and far between. In my opinion, if you are held prisoner with the shameful memories of being a victim and even a perpetrator . . . you may not be able to let it go. But you can let it go forward. Let it go forward in a way that will show people that our peers have potential, which is often thwarted by acts of victimization.

If necessary, work on your public speaking skills while overcoming your shyness in front of preteens and adolescents in the capacity of a role model. In my opinion, this is one of the most effective ways to work through an inability to let go while trying to move forward. When an individual with autism serves as an advocate, he puts his anguish to a greater purpose and it no longer festers.

Forgive Yourself

Some of us have held on to the legacy of shame that our abuse was a self-inflicted punishment for not conforming to expectations or refusing to mature out of naïveté after repeated victimization. I acknowledge that flaunting prominent erections in math class and farting on purpose were not conducive to avoiding bullying. But as an adult, I understand and have forgiven myself for such attention-hungry stunts. The expectations for peer acceptance in childhood were not realistic or fair. Conforming would entail dressing in a manner that was as unnatural as wearing a constricting Halloween costume every day and faking a foreign accent. Most individuals with Asperger's syndrome have made an effort to be "normal" at least once in our childhoods. Conforming never seemed to work and even tended to make things worse. Much of your inappropriate behavior may have also come about during times when earning positive attention from your neurotypical peers was impossible. Any type of attention that would validate your existence was better than being ignored. In other words, it is time to stop blaming yourself for occurrences of bullying and understand the myth of "self-infliction" will always justify suffering for your much younger peers who are currently struggling.

When my first book was published, I was offered an amazing gift in the sense that I learned the true reason why we are targeted. Some of my former victimizers came out of the woodwork as I reluctantly accepted their Facebook requests. Then they apologized for having ever victimized me even though I barely remembered some of their wrongdoing. Their reasoning for this decade-old abuse was very surprising. They brought up stories about disastrous home lives and childhoods filled with abominable anguish. Childhood should be the one time of someone's life when they are sheltered from this brutality. But some of my victimizers did not receive too many breaks early in their lives. They scrounged for self-esteem and power wherever they could find it like a mule draining water from the stem of an Arizona cactus. While this does not justify the lingering trauma they have caused you, it should give you some solace to understand that 80 percent of your bullying was never about you.

Seek Out Role Models and Success Stories—and Work to Become One

The media has discovered the issue of bullying and is giving it more airtime. Recently, there was a story about a boy who has not had much mercy in his life from day one. He was born with a speech impediment as a result of a brain hemorrhage and has the quirk of always wearing a suit, fedora, and tie. He was also not endowed with athletic ability and could only serve as the water boy for a youth football team. When his teammates learned that classmates had been picking on him, they held a "Danny Day" in which everyone else dressed up in a suit, too. I also find comfort in watching other facets of progress such as Pink's music video "Raise Your Glass" and Taylor Swift's "Mean." More stars and personalities in popular culture are revealing that they were once the freaks and misfits who are now being lionized for their "abnormality."

Growing up, I always strained to find an adult version of me who is a quintessential ocean gemstone that has been incessantly polished by hardship. Someone who could explain the difference between qualities of Asperger's that warranted acceptance and behaviors that would need improvement. Now, as an adult, I am working to be that role model for others.

When I stood on the stage of my former middle school, where I once performed grotesque gyrations in a musical production of *Lumberjacks and Weddingbelles*, I now donned a court jester hat with jingle bells affixed like the malevolent troll in the Stephen King anthology *Cat's Eye*. It felt wonderful to finally flaunt and glorify the same weirdness that once invited abuse. Every audience I speak to includes some kids who are receptive to my messages and begin to see their peers in a new light. There are sometimes children with Asperger's who have tears rolling down their faces. One day, a group of my young peers approached me after a presentation and said, "Thank you for sticking up for us and not letting go." Perhaps the solution for all of our residual trauma is to not let go but hold on for dear life and put it toward something constructive. Maybe not necessarily as an Anti-Bullying Activist or mentor for youths with Asperger's, but something else just as profound. Embrace your passions and your difference. Show the world that these are strengths, not weaknesses. And most important, use your talents to change the world.

THERE IS NO SUCH THING AS A FREE LUNCH

While I did not lose my virginity at a young age or go down the path of teen parenthood that has been publicized (and discouraged) through reality TV of late, I did succeed in giving birth to something in my late twenties—something that would take on a life of its own and place demands on my lifestyle for many years to come.

It was an inanimate but anthropomorphic being. Each month it grew hungrier, and the only thing that satisfied it was wads of cash. Like an evil version of Pac-Man, all it wanted to do was consume my money before settling back into brief dormancy. The amount of currency needed to sate it once every month started out very reasonable, but there were six more of these hungry beings that all seized a pound of flesh. It is a beast known as "Credit Card Debt!"

Money has always been one of my special interests, and the seeds of my problem were planted as far back as five years of age. Coins had always stimulated me, and not just because they had the ability to procure video arcade binges or other endorphin-releasing activities. I liked their perpetual coldness and texture as they fell through my fingers like golden sand. The blue toy cash register from my childhood still gathers dust in the basement. But for years, I relished the *chinging* sound whenever a nickel, dime, or quarter was placed inside the device. When the change accrued to ten dollars, there was always a massive *chang* sound as the aluminum slot opened up . . . freeing my treasure chest. Then the process would start over and send me to the moon.

As is often the case with Asperger's, one obsession begat several others as I started watching daily episodes of *Duck-Tales* on the Disney Channel (before it became a tween cesspool). Many episodes featured Scrooge McDuck literally jumping headfirst off a diving board into a cavernous room of gold coins. (As proven in a recent episode of *Family Guy*, an ocean of change would form a concrete-like surface and the average human would probably break every vertebra in his neck!)

The pool of coins swelled from a "special interest" to a festering illusion of power. As a teenager, I developed the bad habit of carrying around substantial amounts of cash for absolutely no reason other than to imitate the "Made Men" I saw on film. They always had a smug look on their faces and toted wallets that were flush with cash. The only thing that killed this fantasy and infused an explosion of common sense was when nearly one hundred dollars was stolen from my perpetually unlocked gym locker. The arrogance diminished when the rest of my day was spent sobbing, as my parents vacillated between sympathy and rage over the theft. "Oh God, Jesse! You really need to wise up one of these days!"

As a result of living in an upper-middle-class family and having a strong work ethic, I was never lacking in money. It certainly never went toward clothes, between my family owning a clothing store and maintaining much of the same wardrobe since my high school years. Like the acorn stash of a greedy squirrel, most of it was funneled into the bank, and my expenses rarely reached beyond age-inappropriate diversions such as trips to Hyde Park Roller Magic. An absence of car payments, insurance, romantic partners, and other adult considerations always left an abundance of disposable income.

It started off innocuously enough. The first card was an extension of my local bank with a credit limit of four thousand dollars. With it, I experienced the thrill of financial liberation. One piece of plastic could finance a pilgrimage back to Ocean City, Maryland, where I could manipulate animatronic items in the boardwalk shooting gallery using a laser speck from a toy rifle. The second and third cards lulled me to sleep as I recreated the Kevin Spacey scene from the 1999 film *American Beauty*. Instead of creased rose petals, there were DVD compilations, roller skates, and nigiri sushi rolls floating from a new portal in the ceiling. The price for overindulgence is always a devastating, Chernobyl-like crash whose shock waves continue to reverberate. As I was beginning to discover, adulthood leaves us susceptible to greater messes that take longer to clean up.

It also did not help that the aggregate beast appealed to one of my other special interests. I have always loved sending out large amounts of mail that require a forty-something-cent stamp to propel it across the country like a paper courier pigeon! Checks and other forms of stationery were also titillating enough for me to continue embroiling myself in this mess. I settled on checks with pictures of Disney characters to make it more enjoyable to send out mail. Food shopping for my family had always been a cherished part of my routine, but now it was becoming even more joyful. It was now my ritual to swipe the balance of a week's worth of groceries on a card with a smaller balance, give my mother the change, and pocket the rest of the cash to finance another week of my playboy-like lifestyle without the sexual adventures.

My family's den had turned into a demolished rain forest of old statements, not to mention the mail offering consolidation deals or debt negotiating services. Even with my profound lack of common sense, I knew not to bother with those. Consolidation companies make the monthly payment more affordable, but it is still like chipping away at a granite mountain using the chisel from a pottery studio. More mail followed, as the credit card companies grew wise enough to turn off my open faucet of debt. There was also mail informing me that applications for new credit cards has been declined due to my "outstanding balances on existing cards." A credit card company closed at least one account after the old card expired, and all that I was left with was a two-cent rectangle of plastic. The possessions and adventurous sprees had also been drained of fantastic novelty with the aching of a withdrawal-like crash.

The credit card statements with their astronomical balances were often littered around the house because filing the storm of paperwork proved to be a nuisance. In reality, however, I probably wanted to get caught. There were murmurs from the den one night, *Oh, my God! He may be in really bad shape!*

My parents had opened up one of the discarded credit card statements with a balance of more than three thousand dollars. The shit began to hit the fan in steady increments that night as I fessed up that there were six more slips with similar balances. The next month's round of statements made their way to the mailbox, and I collected them as promised. For the first time in two years I actually did the math. The calculator read a couple hundred dollars over twenty-five thousand.

The one-way monorail to Financial Ruin rarely happens overnight, and the beginning is such a smooth ride. Who can resist a colorful piece of plastic that is a problem solver and gushing faucet of hedonistic pleasures? My countless projects also demanded the resources of seven credit cards, especially when the plan started to disintegrate. The reasonable man or woman knows when it is time to just move on, which is never me. I hurled snowball-sized clumps of money until the project had run its course. The list of expenses always grew out of hand with another blank, plastic check to pick up the slack. But the main reason is because I was smarter than everyone else in the world. And it was always someone else's fault no matter how ridiculous the purchase.

For a long time, I blamed the schools who fired me from substitute teaching assignments over benign mistakes that "forced" me to turn to credit cards to compensate for loss of income. I blamed the credit card companies for creating a legalized form of loan sharking. In my most pathetic moments, I even raged against TV producers for not promoting my endeavors after I spent a small fortune trying to wine and dine them with twenty-dollar boxes of handcrafted Moonstruck chocolates. My father explained repeatedly that I was flushing my money down the toilet because expensive gifts would not make a difference in whether or not my messages were received. But I always justified my lunacy. "I know that! But it sure is going to help!"

A once-a-month tempest raged on in the Saperstein household with my father always angry about my failure to pay anything beyond the minimum payments. The lecture always remained the same along with my monosyllabic answers.

"Jesse, you're a smart guy. What is it that you do not understand? Credit card companies love people like you! You are going to be in debt for the rest of your life if you do not start paying off the principal."

I would always explain to my dad that the minimum payments were not so "minimum" anymore due to the astronomical balances on each card. In fact, the smallest payments I could make on the collective minimum payments from seven cards accumulated to at least five hundred dollars a month! My new job as a dishwasher at an autism school was also not enough money to shave off slivers of the principal. One day, my dad decided he had enough and said, "Look, Jesse. I am going to speak to my accountant to see if we have any other options."

Once in a while, I play the "Twenty-Five-Thousand-Dollar Game" and think of how much money I actually spent—a quarter of a hundred thousand dollars. It is harmless entertainment to fantasize about what else this money could have been spent on that I at least would have remembered. For a couple of winters I could have flown to Florida over twenty times where I would have walked around aimlessly for a day and flown home after sampling the seventy-degree, subtropical weather. An insatiable longing for 1980s nostalgia could have possessed me to build a mini Never-Never Land in my family's basement. A parade of UPS trucks would pull into my driveway wheeling vintage games like *Donkey Kong* and *Galaga* purchased from obscure Midwestern warehouses. In reality, the spree was so intense that I barely remember how long it took to spend this money or 80 percent of what was purchased.

The twenty-five-thousand-dollar debt technically still exists, but it is no longer seven screaming infants that are arrested in development. I am one of the fortunate individuals with Asperger's syndrome who have a supportive family. My father agreed to take out a twenty-five-thousand-dollar home equity loan on the house to torpedo my entire debt. He also explained that if it was not paid back, then we could potentially lose our home. Four out of my seven cards were cancelled forever and promptly met their doom in the paper shredder. It is now an almost daily custom to receive advertisements from credit card companies that grovel like harpies singing songs of luxury and begging me to ride another foaming tsunami of credit.

Check Yourself Before You Wreck Yourself

The adult world is filled with temptations, and you might find yourself swept into reckless decisions. You might be drawn to enjoy the fruits of extravagance even if it takes borrowed money to accomplish this goal. But do not accelerate too much especially if something appears to give you temporary wings. The mythological figure Icarus met his untimely fate by ignoring warnings and flew too close to the sun with his man-made wings constructed out of feathers and wax. Similarly, if you're not careful, credit cards can give you wings of plastic.

In addition, trouble is often caused by an inflated belief in one's intelligence and inability to absorb the devastating experiences of others. I knew people in severe credit card debt whose mess was caused by purchasing jewelry and other lavish gifts for unrequited love interests. They bought the newest, most expensive car instead of a decent used model. Others became addicted to the adrenaline that comes from shopping on the QVC and Home Shopping Network channels. (This has never been my vice of choice, but different strokes for different folks to fill different voids.) In each case, the extravagant spending was fueled by the belief that the spender was smarter, more capable, and more sensible than everyone else. Irrational, to say the least.

If you're headed down this terrible path, there are things you can do to regain control of the situation. Here is a list of tips that have worked for me and others I truly care about:

■ **Don't let guilt and shame worsen your predicament.** Your guilt will undoubtedly be exacerbated by the unfettered opinions of those in your life who judge you as "reckless" and even "selfish" without offering any advice on how to fix the problem. While there is no way to completely eliminate these feelings of shame, an abundance of negativity is essentially like a rocking chair. Perseverating only on the pain gives you something to do, but it never gets you anywhere.

■ **Consider declaring bankruptcy (if necessary).** Bankruptcy is essentially the gastric bypass surgery of fiscal disaster. In some cases, it is the best option. Consult a financial expert, but do not automatically rule out this path until you've explored how it might help you start over in order to begin to rebuild your life.

■ **Create an emergency fund.** Regardless of whether or not you are in debt, your best investment is to maintain a separate account at a different bank. Try to add a reasonable amount of money each month depending on what you can afford. Some well-intentioned individuals may criticize you for "putting your money to sleep." In reality, you will have a safety cushion that may be used to slough off unexpected setbacks without reaching for the plastic.

■ **Taste the fruits of life.** Sample, but do not gorge. Sip, but do not chug. Frugality may be the less disastrous extreme, but it is important to have some fun with excess income and do things for yourself once in a while. Frugality is also known to backfire into extravagance. Like extreme dieting that deprives a person of every gustatory pleasure, extreme budgeting without occasional respite and small rewards for progress is most likely a recipe for disaster. Even as you are scratching your way back like a battered fighter on a comeback trail, I am hoping you will have the strength to show yourself the generosity that may not always come from someone else. In the summer of 2013, I had paid off my home equity loan two months in advance with an account flush with disposable income. Another friend with Asperger's and I decided to take a trip to my childhood haunt of Wildwood Crest, New Jersey, at a cheap motel. We referred to it as the "Asperger's Summit," and shooting down the alien spacecraft in the retro arcade was just as titillating as any part of my spending spree. Two years earlier, I would have swiped the whole vacation on one of the credit cards and stayed at the most extravagant motel for longer than four days.

■ **Maintain employment or an active lifestyle (or both).** I have noticed that people seem to find trouble when they have too much time on their hands. Therefore, the worst of my debt (and miscellaneous other problems) accumulated when I was in between jobs and filled idle time with "stuff" thanks to a seemingly unlimited supply of credit. When I was steadily employed, the temptation to be frivolous was severely limited based on what it took to generate my own income. In contrast, when my idle hands had nothing to do except type credit card numbers on Amazon.com, my room became an adult toy chest of DVDs, unread books, and other knick-knacks that padded my self-esteem. If a paying job will not come to fruition anytime in the near future, the next best option is to procure some type of volunteer work at least three days a week. When you make yourself accountable to something besides self-gratification, you will be less likely to be pursued by trouble.

■ **Make it fun.** Becoming fiscally sensible should be something that appeals to your Asperger's eccentricities. To help me stay on the right path, I used a battery-operated children's ATM-style piggy bank. After enough money had been stored in there, it was deposited in my savings account. Find a way to make saving money fun for yourself.

■ **Do not try to solve problems with the same strategies that created them.** For a long time, I nursed the erroneous belief that my credit card problems could be eradicated with more cards and cash advances. It was like playing musical chairs with toxic waste as the debt bounced from one card to the other. An inflated ego prevented me from asking for help. Recognize when it's time to cut your losses and try a new strategy to get back on track.

■ **Seek help from trusted experts and friends.** Confronting the problem will not be pretty, especially when you must fess up to your loved ones that you are in trouble. I urge you to identify those people in your life who are worth confiding in because they will help you solve the crisis even after their brief explosion of disgust. Even though you may be experiencing challenges that affect many adults, overcoming the consequences may take much longer due to a lack of resources and your challenges with executive functioning. The proper counselor will take you step by step into recovery, and eventually you will be able to initiate steps on your own.

■ **Use rock bottom as a springboard.** Failure—whether it's financial troubles, employment woes, or other crises in one's life—can be a great motivator. My Descent into Debt was the catalyst that drove me to secure my first full-time job in five years and prove to future employers that I am not a liability.

The transition into adulthood means confronting temptation that levitates like apples from the Garden of Eden. You will be vulnerable to the same mistakes as the neurotypical population, and the hardest part is dealing with the shame that will keep you from taking the required action. Guilt and self-disgust barred me from going to my parents to let them know I was drowning in debt from purchasing such "bare necessities" as Broadway shows to charm dates from Match .com. My family would show anger just like they have in the past over reckless decisions and an inability to learn from previous mistakes. It is critical to prepare yourself for the brief explosion of anger because the next phase will entail a long-term journey of gratification . . . paving the road for solutions.

So don't shut out reality and push off action for another day. Even the smallest changes can help you create powerful momentum toward reclaiming your life.

NOBODY'S FOOL

Plenty of us on the autism spectrum are known for our Boy Scout–like honesty, prompting us to return lost wallets, follow through on our commitments, and naïvely believe that others share our strict code of honor. However, it is important to eventually learn that the rest of the world does not always share our ethical rigor and set of rules.

As a child, I never seemed to learn from my mistakes. Despite having been tormented by a cyberbullying prank back in 1999 for six months, I continued to embrace strangers on the Internet and even fell for another hoax many years later.

Many of us have grown accustomed to being victimized. Over and over, in support groups and among friends, I have heard of Aspies falling prey to scams that range from romantic trysts gone awry, to financial "opportunities" that don't quite pan out the way we'd hoped. In a perfect world, people would not take advantage of others—especially when the "others" are sometimes short on common sense and long on naïveté and gullibility. But we do not live in a perfect world.

We must accept the truth that our naïveté will often lead to us buying the magic beans. Unlike the many adaptations of "Jack and the Beanstalk" (my favorite being the 1967 Hanna-Barbera version), nothing magical usually sprouts from taking the bait. Whenever you are duped or taken advantage of, it is critical to perform an investigation and analyze the carnage like a forensic crime specialist. Were there any red flags that you may have been oblivious to or brushed off? Someone would do us a world of good by creating a book titled *The Encyclopedia of Scams*. The book would be an anthology that chronicles financial scams, elaborate schemes, and people whose vulnerabilities make them a walking target. They have been rolled around by life like a strip of Play-Doh and are now able to share the red flags with probable victims. But until such a book comes to fruition, here are some of the warning signs that have stood out in my experience:

■ **Red Flag 1: Strangers seeking you out as romantic partners.** A devastating online experience (which I described in my previous book, *Atypical*) taught me to be wary of random suitors and unsolicited courtship. For the past few years, I have been receiving Facebook messages from gorgeous women with more curves than a NASCAR speedway. They are sprawled in erotic positions and always seem to see my potential as a willing sex slave or sensitive partner. Their messages, often written in broken English, invite me to email them and suggest we could have a loving relationship.

I have news for all of my peers (myself included). This glamorous photograph and saccharine prose is merely the perfume disguising a cruel ruse. God may have peered from the celestial heavens this morning and anointed you as the Luckiest Person with Asperger's in the Universe. Or perhaps there is some obscure fetish that compels foreign supermodels to develop feverish sexual hunger for men with social challenges. But realistically, there is a much greater chance it is a scam, and you will recognize the signs. You may also receive emails from someone in Nairobi who has inherited his uncle's fortune that is held hostage by an international bank and needs you to transfer money to free the fortune from its fiscal shackles. You will be entitled to receive a percentage of the funding in exchange for your participation. Your biggest red flags are always messages coming from foreign countries and any inquiries for personal information to set the imaginary gears in motion.

■ **Red Flag 2: Someone asking you to pay in order to take an obscure test and/or purchase materials to become part of a new job.** We should strive every day to better ourselves both socially and professionally. But this ambition may become our downfall if we find ourselves paying fees to join a "booming franchise," which is usually code for a pyramid scheme. The only way to earn back the money we invested is to (a) sucker additional saps into purchasing the same worthless franchise, or (b) possess the psychological talents and sales skills to sell off the inventory. Both possibilities are unlikely to happen and we will never see that money again. How would you feel if your local supermarket agreed to hire you as a checkout cashier but demanded you pay them fifty dollars a week for a solid month before you started to earn money? Chances are you would want to tell them to do something to themselves that is not anatomically possible! The same logic should apply everywhere else. If you have doubts about whether something is legitimate, then please take the route of asking some of your neurotypical supporters who are older or wiser. Or perhaps your Asperger's role models who are seasoned by past deception.

■ **Red Flag 3: A sequence of sympathetic tales or excuses.** Sympathy is a powerful drug and when combined with manipulation, it bubbles into a dangerous cocktail. We have probably been guilty of such deception ourselves, from time to time. Some of us manipulated teachers into excusing us from an assignment by throwing a temper tantrum that rivaled that scene from *The Omen* when the pint-sized Antichrist, Damien, is driven to church. But it is uncommon for our manipulation to have malicious intent, and we foolishly expect others to have the same standards.

You should take a step back and reevaluate friendships where someone is riding a Wave of Woe and consistently asks for money or leniency to buffer this misery. Those with Asperger's are more vulnerable to Catfishing scams in which a faceless cyber stranger poses as a romantic interest and wards off your first face-to-face meeting with a sequence of flamboyant tales. When your mysterious new friend battles terminal cancer, financial liquidation, abrupt unemployment, the death of a parent, a car crash, homelessness, and a brutal mugging in the span of just two months . . . it is time to take another look. There is the unlikely possibility that this individual is genuinely living the martyred life of a heroine from a Hollywood dark comedy. Be that as it may, you will save yourself a lot of future misery (and cash) by not augmenting your own problems with their endless crises.

■ **Red Flag 4: Someone threatening to kick you out of the "club" or close the deal if you show reluctance.** Sara is an older member of my Asperger's support group. Life has not given her too many breaks, and her lined face suggests far more than her fifty-one years. At the end of the 1990s, she was offered the "chance of a lifetime" to be part of an Internet start-up company that would "take Silicon Valley by storm." The last step involved boarding a plane to meet her new partner in Los Angeles where she would relinquish a chunk of her life savings for seed money. A few days prior to the flight brought a tsunami of better judgment when Sara informed the partner of her decision to consult with a lawyer. The partner began screaming at her over the phone for being disloyal and threatened to terminate the deal. She wisely slammed the phone down to mute his desperate protests.

> *When you cross that bridge, my friend,*
> *the ghost is gone . . . his power ends!*
> —Walt Disney's *Legend of Sleepy Hollow*

I believe it was the self-deprecating Groucho Marx who once said, "I would not want to belong to a club that accepted me as a member." But many of us are emerging from childhoods of chronic isolation and rejection. With that said, potential victimizers are talented at sensing such hot buttons and push them like a six-year-old running amok in his first arcade. This is how the infamous sociopath Bernie Madoff ended up ruining people's lives at the tune of fifty billion dollars. He made them feel like part of something exclusive and special. If people dared to ask questions, he had the power to shut them out with the velvet ropes. A genuine person will not use intimidation to get you to go along with the plan.

■ **Red Flag 5: Purchasing items over the phone with your credit card.** We sometimes forget that it is "our" phone and nobody has the right to impose upon our time unless we allow it to happen. Telemarketers are not James Bond–style villains or Sarah Palin. They are probably decent people struggling to make a living just like everyone else in this recovering recession and may despise what they must do in order to pay rent. But this does not mean we have to fall for the sales pitch. You should never, ever purchase something over the phone *when a stranger calls.* (The last four words of that sentence are the title of a horror movie, but I believe the plot had to do with a serial killer and not telemarketers.) Many offers are perfectly legitimate, and we are the ones responsible for taking the bait. Others are less than honorable and cynically prey on gullibility. The most brazen of scam artists evade all legal responsibility by hiding under the sovereignty of their own nation. If you find yourself falling for anything over the phone and fear the rudeness of hanging up in mid-conversation, one solution is to purchase the Gotta Go Machine. This clever device simulates the sound of a baby crying, a dog barking, traffic cacophony, and other din that will give you an excuse to extricate yourself from a phone conversation. Or simply practice saying, "I'm sorry, but I have to go now."

■ **Red Flag 6: A parasitic relationship consisting of one-sided favors.** Some of us are starved for social connections and will take what is available. We may devalue ourselves as human beings, and our standards become very low as far as whom we allow in our lives. You may pick up ticks along for the ride that engorge themselves with your generosity. They will not move on until you wise up. Relationships should not be sustained by favors, nor should one expect something in return as the price of helping someone else. When today's favors always make the transition into tomorrow's duties, it is time to reevaluate this one-sided friendship and finally embrace your worth as a human being.

If you do choose the rocky path of loaning someone your hard-earned money, the best thing to do is have him or her sign a piece of paper stating they owe you this sum. Insist on paying with a check so there is a record of this transaction and evidence that the debt actually exists. Do not lend out money that you cannot easily afford to lose, and close the bank vault until the first debt is paid back.

Learning the Hard Way

My old hiking partner on the Appalachian Trail said something very profound with regard to these painful learning experiences. He told me, "Whenever something bad happens to you in life, the best way to keep it from happening again is to just blame yourself." This was back in 2005. I was only twenty-two and this friend was forty-eight. He had half a century's worth of life experience, but I was still too immature to take his words seriously. They actually angered me. How can it be our fault when someone takes advantage of our Asperger's-induced innocence?

My literary agent also said, "The world can be a hot kitchen.

If we do not grow more seasoned toward some unchangeable realities, then we are fated to get burnt repeatedly."

■ **Accept your mistake, and move onward.** When you find yourself duped and deceived . . . blaming yourself *does not* mean that you deserve these consequences. But the repercussions for not taking some responsibility for your mistakes will guarantee being taken advantage of in the same manner. Not acknowledging the red flags in retrospect shall allow them to go over your head again in the future. Prepare yourself far in advance that some scams and fraudulent friends might continue to pursue you, and learn from the experiences of others whenever possible.

■ **Share your hard-won wisdom.** Let's serve as role models to shave off some of the anguish that our younger peers would normally face through bitter experiences or those with more challenging cases of naïveté who have not yet reached the plateau we have mounted. Some of these disasters will be circumvented with our combined, solicitous intervention.

■ **Seek out help.** We tend to go wrong by listening to our pride instead of turning to our support system to ask for advice. Or perhaps we fear someone berating our gullibility instead of offering deserved praise for seeking their perspective. One of these days, we will be able to look out for ourselves with minimal support, but it will not be tomorrow or the day after that. Until that day arrives, allow your neurotypical friends to hold your hand a little longer. Or at the very least, learn from your more seasoned peers who have been scarred by deception.

■ **Watch your step.** I sometimes find it useful to think of humanity as an abundance of flowers and innocuous weeds. And there are always going to be a few random patches of poison ivy mixed into the vegetation. It is not everywhere, but it is abundant enough to make our lives miserable after grazing our flesh. Poison ivy has been granted defense mechanisms even though its survival serves no purpose for mankind. It clings to a host tree, or a fence, and takes up space wherever else it thrives. It glistens with superficial beauty in the summer's gloaming hours with the beauty of a stained-glass window. If this vile weed imposes itself into your life, it would be wise to hold on to the hard lesson after the flaming blisters finally recede. And shame on us if we choose to roll around like a demented, feral child in a patch of strange weeds after the first experience!

■ **Move on.** Anger is a natural response, and I am the last person who should lecture you about letting go of toxic energy. But after the anger eventually subsides or at least recedes into a shallow tide, it would be in your best interest to stop feeling like a victim long enough to analyze the learning experience. Unlike our childhood memories of being bullied, it is usually not a personal conspiracy against you but rather a reflection of the person who pulled off the scam. They lack a conscience or treat the operation like a business where the "customer" deserves to pay a price for their foolishness. If you are fortunate, you might even find a way to laugh about it, in time, and recommit yourself to the cause of not getting fooled again.

WALKING AWAY
FROM TROUBLE

Instinct told me he was headed for disaster. But he didn't agree, and he argued his case with the greatest of eloquence. My attempts to change his mind went nowhere, and I could not decide on a course of action.

"Why put the videos online at all?" I asked him. This was the obvious question. By this time, he'd uploaded twenty-some videos to his own channel on YouTube. Cubby said he had worked hard to accomplish what he had, and he wanted to share the results with other chemists who might want to do something similar.

—John Elder Robison, *Raising Cubby*

A few years ago, while struggling with my health and weight, I decided to emulate an energetic senior citizen in my community, who walks multiple miles every day despite being in her eighties. A local legend, she walks in all types of weather and even has thousands of fans on Facebook thanks to being such a neighborhood inspiration.

While lapses in health are common among people of all abilities, my problems were exacerbated when my neuroses and rituals attached to bad habits like petrified barnacles. The first step of one's recovery is always admitting you have a problem, and the moment of rock bottom is different for all individuals. The Epiphany from Hell washed over me in the shower upon noticing that my genitalia were completely obscured by a protruding stomach. This nightmare did not happen overnight and was accelerated by a compulsion to remain faithful to the clean plate club, especially in restaurants with generous portions. Leaving food on one's plate meant letting someone throw it in the garbage. Taking it home also meant surrendering to one of those plastic foam containers that poison our environment with nonbiodegradable toxins!

Some of my walks lasted as much as seven miles. I would sometimes hike to a favorite diner (not the best idea since a large meal would negate the effects of the walk). One day in mid-February, I decided to wear the new ski mask that my father brought home from our family's clothing store. Even though it was not that cold out, I brought it along because it looked really cool, like one of those phantasm monsters from *Pac-Man*. Even with my Asperger's, I knew the foolishness of wearing such a garment inside a bank or any public place. But walking around in the middle of winter seemed harmless enough.

A police cruiser came to a slow stop with the crunching of gravel as the tall and wiry officer leaned his head out and asked, "Are you all right? What are you doing out here? What is in your pockets?"

I pulled out a phone charger and an assortment of crumpled-up tissue fluff that fell to the pavement like snowflakes. "Just taking a walk back to the diner. Is something wrong, Officer?"

"No, there is nothing wrong. We have just been getting some 911 phone calls from the community that a suspicious man has been walking around wearing a ski mask. I mean, you know how people are these days."

I nodded and said, "I understand, Officer. It is just the times we are living in lately."

He said, "I am going to get out of the car and look up your ID if that is all right."

As my information was punched into the computer, my heightened, Asperger's spidey senses heard the distinct klakkety-klacks of his police laptop, as he undoubtedly came to the conclusion that I was not a threat to anyone in the community, aside from maybe myself.

"All right, sir. You are all set. I am sorry to bother you, Mr. Saperstein." He smiled and extended his hand. But I was not finished with the conversation.

"I am just curious whether this is going to become a regular thing? After all, I plan to take walks like this in the future!"

He assured me there was nothing to worry about and drove off. Judging from many similar encounters, I knew this was not the end. But I just thought there would be more of a grace period especially considering I had removed the ski mask.

Less than a half an hour later, I almost tripped over a cardboard box lying in the middle of the road that contained a cookbook along with a receipt addressed to a residence across town. Assuming it fell off a postal truck, I began carrying it with intentions of driving to the address that evening. The individual with Asperger's syndrome is often a salvage expert. If something is lost, then you must find it and return it to its rightful owner. The accolades from these feats of heroism should serve to buffer some of the more painful realities and fear from society. Sometimes we are rewarded, and other times our good deeds come with consequences.

Another police cruiser pulled up beside me, and I assumed it was the same man. Perhaps he returned with plans of giving me a ride home to kill off the incoming batch of hysterical phone calls. But it was a different officer this time.

"What can I do for you, Officer? I am just heading to a diner down the road." I told him the name of my hometown when asked.

He looked at me condescendingly and asked as though I were a lost child, "Aren't we a little far away from home to be walking in the rain? Furthermore, our station has been receiving 911 calls that someone has been walking around carrying a strange box."

Chances are you have also felt the societal sting from having outbursts in public or employment situations. They fly out of our mouths like black ravens of rage without hesitation. But there are autism angels that take over to hold us back as we mature. Invisible verbal leashes are present that grow more taut from negative experiences and lessons learned the hard way. This is why it is so important to work to understand and be part of the neurotypical world. There will be mishaps and blunders that come out of making yourself more vulnerable, but their haunting penalties will serve a vital purpose when it comes to future misunderstandings. *When did taking a walk become a crime in this world? You should tell whoever keeps calling you to get a life!* But I did not say this even though five years ago I probably would have felt justified in relating my frustration. Something held it back.

"Actually, Officer, I do this kind of stuff all the time. Let me pull up my web page, and I will show you what I mean. One time, I walked all the way from Georgia to Maine for 2,174 miles. And the box is something I found in the middle of the street with a book inside."

The officer viewed a slideshow with a look of pity on his face. After all, those were the days when I was literally in the shape of an Olympic athlete from walking fifteen miles a day for seven months, sporting a natural suntan to boot. An impulse also prompted me to hand him my business card and find the web page about having Asperger's syndrome and my first memoir, *Atypical*.

"This card should explain everything, Officer. I can show you what is inside the box if you want."

He continued, "That won't be necessary. I think you have explained to me quite well what the situation is and why you are walking. I thank you for being so open to talking with me about it."

I replied, "You can hang on to this card if you would like. It has all of my contact information including my cell phone. You will probably get calls like this in the future from the community, and it is not fair for you to have to drive all the way out here for no reason. Are you aware this is the second time I have been stopped by a police officer in less than two hours? Maybe you could call this number to make sure it is only me? I mean . . . I have a right to try and lose weight!" With that statement, I jiggled my bulging stomach.

The officer also shook his stomach and said, "I know what you mean! I have that right, as well!" When the moment of awkward male bonding had concluded, the officer said, "I do not need your card. We have a duty to respond to all calls no matter how ridiculous they are. And if I notice it is you walking, then I will just say, 'Oh! There goes Jesse again' and will drive on by."

The encounter ended and we parted ways with an exchange of mutual respect. He was one of those cherished people who radiate with empathy and mercy. They also have the ability to distinguish a threat from benign weirdness. Later on, I drove to the address on the box, which turned out to be a somewhat dilapidated house. A woman answered the door. Without being rude or polite, she grabbed the box and said a monotone "thank you" before shutting the door in my face.

"Here's My Card"

My business card has turned into a useful tool in these situations. The information about my public speaking career essentially screams out, "My name is Jesse A. Saperstein. I have Asperger's syndrome!" If you are an individual who is unable to communicate during periods of misunderstandings and confrontations you cannot diffuse on your own, it may be a good idea to also carry copies of your special card. The card could state your diagnosis as well as unusual characteristics associated with your mild autism. We were taught from a very early age that the quickest way to enhance one's intellectual prowess is to ask a lot of questions. But in the adult world, there are fewer questions and more actions sparked by spontaneous fear. Therefore, it may be a good idea to practice the art of disclosure, which has allowed me to reduce fear in my community. It has also led to similar interactions with authority figures that have been positive and brief in their confrontational nature. It is critical to train police officers on how to recognize citizens with developmental disabilities and react appropriately, but much of this success will fall on our shoulders.

Becoming Aware of How Others See You

As we age into adulthood, our naïveté tends to linger for longer than our neurotypical peers. We often fail to grasp how the world views our harmless behaviors. Antics are no longer cute or dismissed as harmless. We may also tend to be egocentric and fail to grasp other individuals' points of view. Harmlessness takes on the scent of malice, and some of us act like playful dogs in a perpetual state of arrested development. We are like grown Rottweilers who jump on people's laps, thinking it will still be viewed as adorable.

You may also be the target of police intervention when your quirks elicit fear from community members who are not aware of your diagnosis. These consequences are not a personal conspiracy against you. They are part of living in an adult world where rules and precautions are necessary.

As a child, I was unable to understand why my parents tried to expunge any quality that deviated from normalcy. They might as well have been beating a dusty rug with a tennis racket. The fine particles rain down like asbestos, but there is always a little bit left. More will accumulate soon. At first, I thought they were rejecting this innocent uniqueness. *You need to stop acting so weird.* But in reality, they were protecting me. They know enough about human nature to understand that differences are not always embraced in society. My parents' premonitions were hardly irrational considering they have had to field several phone calls from police departments over the years.

When you are at the center of such misunderstandings, it is critical to keep a few things in mind. This is not personal. Part of the transition into adulthood is trying to understand this fear-mongering from the neurotypical public is no longer personal. It is not a conspiracy against you as a person and is merely a consequence of the times we live in these days. Most important, you will find that the amazing thing about showing respect is how it comes back to you like a boomerang of benevolence.

Times Have Changed

When I was a child, there did not seem to be such suspicion directed toward those who fail to fit the norm. Mine was the last generation to play outside until the streetlights came on, and CNN was not a twenty-four-hour Fear Fest with lurid tales about kidnappers and other predators. We never had video games featuring thugs beating innocent civilians to death with blunt objects before stealing their vehicles. And for most of elementary school, our class was sent home with catalogues so we could sell wrapping paper to neighborhood houses. We ignored the advice of going along with another person and could have very well been abducted by pedophiles! Parents and educators are much more cautious now. As irrational and unfair as it may seem, this is the nature of society these days, and fear is displaced toward our population. We can butt against these realities like a manic bulldog or we can accept reality.

How Weird Is Too Weird?

Survival in the neurotypical world is dependent on a tapestry of treaties and compromises. Perhaps it is prudent to run down this checklist or devise a similar one of your own:

☐ Does this behavior or public ritual make you happy or enrich your life?

☐ Are you choosing to hold on because letting go seems like the equivalent of death?

☐ As harmless as your actions may be, do they frequently push hot buttons and solicit common fears?

☐ Are you taking unnecessary steps to exaggerate your oddness in an attempt to garner attention?

☐ Is there any room for compromise if letting go altogether seems impossible?

I look back on that February day and realize so much trouble could have been avoided if I had just worn a regular hat instead of a ski mask. The weather conditions of that day did not necessitate a ski mask. I chose this wintry attire because of a need to stand out and draw attention to myself. Now I know better.

Similarly, while watching *The Simpsons Movie*, I let my excitement lead me into some questionable conduct. Without pausing to consider the comfort zone of others, I ran down the aisle before the movie started, exclaiming, "I have been waiting my entire life for this movie!"

Along with my verbal outburst, there was a spectacle of hand flapping and foot pounding as I found one of the empty seats. Some people looked amused, others were mortified, only one or two were cautiously clapping, and some probably wished they had the will to do exactly the same thing. But most looked offended. A young woman turned around and said, "We just want to say that we are all very happy for you. But you had better not do anything like that when the movie actually starts!"

The next day, my father and sister were driving to the train station when a popular radio DJ was talking about her weekend activities.

"I took my kids to see *The Simpsons Movie* on Sunday night when all of a sudden this man comes running down the aisle, ranting about how he has been waiting his whole life for the movie or something. I had thought all of the crazies got it out of their system on Friday night and whoever that was should be a hermit!"

Dad and Dena exchanged a knowing look.

I did not get into trouble, which seemed to justify the stunt at the time. After all, consequences often dictate our actions. But at this late hour, it becomes clear that the absence of repercussions was merely dumb luck. What if the planets and other celestial matter had aligned in a different pattern? What if there had been a police officer there—one who was not inclined to indulge my quirks? Or what if the staff decided to kick me out and ruin what should have been a perfect night? Looking back, I can see that I was lucky. But it's best not to rely on luck.

It would not surprise me if you have also had a rocky start to your adulthood and at least a few awkward incidents when your behavior went a bit over the line. The greatest thing we can do is forgive ourselves for making mistakes along with learning new strategies to avoid similar episodes of boundary testing and misunderstandings in the future. Here's my list of lessons. You might want to add some of your own, too.

- Confide the fact that you have Asperger's if you get the sense that someone is uncomfortable. Then ask if there is anything you may do to make them more comfortable or if they have any questions.

- Understand that some of the disapproval from authority figures and less sensitive members of society might seem personal, but it is not the same as the bullying that you may have endured as a child. In the adult world, most people mature into a live-and-let-live attitude and any superficial mistreatment of others is spawned from fear.

■ Solicit the opinions of trusted family and friends. You should not have to rely solely on common sense or lessons learned firsthand.

■ Identify places where your eccentricities and rituals are welcome. Friends' houses, support groups, and other "safe spaces" where everyone is aware of your quirks and habits, and where you can be yourself without censoring (while still being respectful, safe, and considerate toward others, of course).

■ Conversely, identify places where awkward humor and excess peculiarities *will not* be appreciated. The most obvious example would be any airport, where anything out of the ordinary is perceived as a threat. This is universal around the world for everyone. It is also not a vendetta against the beautiful enigma of Asperger's. Personally, I have found that the greatest strategy within any Kingdom of Walking on Eggshells is to pretend you are a cyborg that has been developed by the Special Government Forces to only respond to routine questions in a voice devoid of personality and humor. If this helps you stay in line, give it a try.

Part of growing into adulthood is learning to adapt to new situations. No one is suggesting that we give up every aspect of our uniqueness. That would be impossible (and not a good idea). But some of our quirks and habits are security blankets from the past that we no longer truly need to hold on to.

Every once in a while, it is critical to clean out one's closet just a little bit and throw out what no longer works. If you cannot let it go entirely, consider shaving it down with a compromise. My most flamboyant rituals have been pushed so far on a back burner that they are nearly invisible. As for your eccentric behaviors, I am not sure what they are or if they stir up irrational fear in your communities or places that do not know your true character. But with a bit of effort, you will find the balance between fitting in and being yourself.

FAMILY MATTERS

I have an older brother who is autistic. While we grew up, it was hard. He got a lot more attention than I did, and I couldn't understand why. He would do things, the same things I would do, and he wouldn't get in trouble and my parents would always say, You know better. I never understood why he didn't get in trouble but I did. We didn't get along then because I had a lot of resentment towards him. But when we were at school I would always stick up for him, though. He would get bullied, and I always stuck up for him. I would never let anyone bully him. That drew us together. When I went away for school, I became closer to everyone, so that was great. Right now, he's battling cancer so that has really drawn us closer. It's made me appreciate him and who he is. And I love him and love that he is my brother.

—Nicole Fishwick, sibling of someone with Asperger's
syndrome

Nobody really forgets . . . do they? What are some of your memories growing up if you happened to share your world with siblings? It is not unheard of to have siblings who are also on the autism spectrum whether or not they choose to accept it. But it is even more common to have at least one neurotypical sibling who had to share your world that was marked by signature quirks and behaviors that affected your family dynamic. Time has probably healed some of the pain, but it would be naïve to believe that it is not necessary to address underlying issues . . . resentment . . . misunderstandings . . . and residual grudges. Adulthood should be a time of healing between you and your siblings.

Autism can rattle families to the core, and yet the issues are often the same as any family with "typical children." It is not totally uncommon for one's seven-year-old sibling to increase the decibel level of obnoxiousness when their older brother or sister turns ten years old. Aside from a rare faction with a *Village of the Damned*–like stoicism . . . most children are Walking Turbine Engines that greedily consume attention as their fuel. The neurotypical sibling may carry on for a little while, but then knock it off when the threat of a time-out is administered, followed by the promise of just as much attention when they turn eight. But a sibling on the autism spectrum may not respond to such intervention. The temper tantrum increases like a feeding frenzy of desire. There is a need for acknowledgment and the same level of celebration. The cries escalate into wails followed by bloodcurdling screams. The other guests stop serenading the "Child of the Hour" and focus on the drama unfolding. The birthday is ruined and bitterness accumulates in the alcoves of your sibling's memory.

This may not be your specific memory, but I would bet it is someone else's who grew up with one of your peers. And I am sure there were similar experiences that may have taken place at a museum, movie theater, or someplace else. Perhaps your sensory issues prevented your family from enjoying typical outings such as movies and plays. Between your parents, there was not always enough attention to go around because autism tends to consume energy like a cyclone at the peak of its power.

Maybe you are an only child. Perhaps autism has diluted in various forms and intensities to at least one other sibling. Or maybe you also have at least one sibling who was born neurotypical. Chances are that all of you are carrying excess baggage that floats to the surface like buoyant parcels from the doomed *Titanic*. Ancient artifacts of childhood yore, residual grudges, and glimmers of respect and euphoria bob to the surface on a regular basis. Adulthood will hopefully be your time to put things away and build on your relationship.

My sister, Dena, came into this world on the evening of October 31, 1984. It was always a novelty to have a sister born on the greatest day of the year for many individuals with Asperger's syndrome. Her birthday celebrations were like Tim Burton fantasies in which the house was smothered with artificial cobwebs and other tidbits of Halloween nostalgia. During a rare moment of bonding, we turned our tree-infested backyard into a haunted house used to entertain the neighborhood children. I hid in a tree and growled at kids like a common lycanthrope. For a girl born on Halloween, she has an unusual fear of horror films that lingered long after most other kids desensitize themselves at sleepovers with movies about homicidal, sentient dolls. Unlike me, she has never found horror to be thrilling or liberating, like a psychological narcotic.

Most older brothers find their sister's weaknesses and dangle it in front of her face like Van Helsing taunting vampires with a crucifix. When I realized the extent of her fears, I insisted on playing the most disturbing horror movies while she was in the living room, out of spite. She scrambled to find the remote control, which was stealthily concealed in the folds of the couch. I followed in the footsteps of many an older brother, including my own father, who used my aunt's favorite doll as creepy collateral damage.

While I did not put that much creative energy into torturing Dena, I baited her for the same reason that George Herbert Leigh Mallory summited Mount Everest: because she was there. Her temper tantrums were easily provoked, and sometimes it took next to nothing for a no-holds-barred meltdown.

I felt a bitterness toward Dena because her social skills were not chained by a social disability. I watched from the sidelines as she propelled relentlessly through every new phase of dating relationships and road trips with friends. I, on the other hand, lived vicariously through the images from Plato's Cave in the form of TV sitcoms. Reruns of *Saved by the Bell* taught me about life throughout my middle school years and much of high school. Dena was only two grade levels behind me, so we shared school experiences where she inherited the reputation of being related to Jesse Saperstein. One day, I observed her talking to a strange student on the Internet. After learning of our relationship, he asked:

"Oh, my God! Are you weird like him?"

Dena usually defended me when my reputation trickled back down to her, but I could tell that it pained her to be genetically linked to the school weirdo. Most of my sister's friends tolerated me, but I could tell that she was reluctant to bring them over to our house.

Dena possesses an unusual amount of empathy, which is an intrinsic quality that has been augmented by having a brother who is on the autism spectrum. In twenty-nine years, I have never witnessed her saying something malicious about any individual, especially someone struggling with limitations.

Clarity sometimes comes for me and Dena during car rides after picking her up from the Poughkeepsie train station. Adulthood has brought us closer together as we face similar battles with common secrets. We both have scars that are superficial and concealed. They are still very much real . . . but fading every single day. I plead with you to get to know your siblings, and do not give in to the temptation of ignoring past baggage. Go on road trips and experience the silliness and mild debauchery that you might not have bonded over as children.

Both Dena and I have traces of Obsessive Compulsive

Disorder. There was the day I started scratching my ear to clean out some wax residue or relieve an itch. It eventually graduated into an open sore and then crusted over into a scab. I always picked away at fresh scabs with a slightly ragged fingernail until that raw smoothness finally returned followed by that wave of satisfaction. The relief was always temporary, however. The thing would crust over once more as the cycle repeated. I do not know anyone who has died from obsessive skin picking, but hypochondria took over as I worried about blood clots forming in my ear canal and traveling to my brain. One day I revealed this unique addiction to Dena, and she instinctively pulled back her hair to reveal a tiny bald patch and her own secret. It never occurred to me that Dena had suffered for years from a condition known as trichotillomania that is medical jargon for hair pulling. Dena had developed the habit of pulling out parts of her hair one strand at a time and once attended a support group for the condition. While I could never relate to the compulsion of pulling out my hair, it did something for her that was soothing. I could understand she would not bother unless every extracted strand emitted a pinprick surge of adrenaline or calm. I told her about the first time a female police officer pulled me over because my constant ear picking made it look like I was on my cell phone.

Dena answered, "That also happened to someone in my group." We bonded further after that moment and finally stood on common ground.

Dena and I have also bonded over the dogged determination to break the habit and exert control over our own bodies. Then we will deal with what is really bothering us. Our universal issues make the banter easier because they involve employment frustrations, unstable romantic relationships, and obsessive-compulsive tendencies.

Healing the Past and Looking Forward to the Future

■ **Apologize for past transgressions.** It is not fair for you to waste energy dwelling on childhood indiscretions that were fueled by both autism and the prefrontal cortex region of your still developing brain responsible for impulse control. But sometimes an apology for any pain you caused will be a turning point. It is less of an apology and more of an acknowledgment that your autism created moments of anguish for your siblings.

■ **Take an interest in their interests, and vice versa.** I sometimes feel like I have been dropped off in my family by an alien species. Nobody (especially Dena) has ever been able to relate to my interests of 2,174-mile hikes, skydiving, or donating platelets sometimes twice a week. It may bother you that your siblings have never shown any enthusiasm over your life joys. But I wonder whether you have ever tried to relate to their passions? One of the justified criticisms that come from the neurotypical public is how we drone endlessly about our interests without providing any grace period for someone else to talk. *The rule of "Five to Five" should also apply to sibling relationships.* For every five minutes you go on about your interests, it is just as important to give your sibling a chance to talk about what makes them tick.

Your brother may cherish his pastime of watching Red Sox games at Fenway Park when you do not see the point of cheering for a team that (in reality) cares nothing about you as an individual. The team's former losing streak over a period of eight decades had created a tsunami of tears, future fears, and frustration. You might never fully understand the appeal or why your sibling puts so much energy into this "hobby." But you might grow closer by asking and truly listening.

It will take a little bit of effort and stepping outside one's comfort zone, but the result will be new synapses of tolerance and a closer sibling bond.

■ **Flush out old grudges and ancient resentment.** If you and at least one of your siblings fostered intense bitterness during your childhoods, then chances are that these feelings may still exist. I remember talking to Dena about how envious I always was that she ascended to all of her milestones on time. Whether it was going out on dates or vacations with close friends, it never seemed fair that her social interaction was not labored by awkwardness or weekly visits to a speech pathologist.

■ **Stop pushing each other's buttons.** It will be as difficult as weaning yourself off caffeine, but it is important to begin respecting each other's sensitive boundaries. Dena has let me in on some of her struggles—with weight loss, for example— and it has dramatically changed my perspective. Where I once would joke and tease, I have learned to be more sensitive. I now see that we have both been seasoned by hardship and are simultaneously struggling to build our adult lives.

■ **Become a great aunt or uncle.** While it is not unheard of for individuals with Asperger's to marry and have children, it is much more common for our neurotypical siblings to move on to this life phase. There will be new additions to your family in the form of a screaming infant that will rise to various phases of development at a steady pace. Any old resentment or tensions may melt away as you find yourself caring for this beautiful young person. You will find a lion's share of purpose when it comes to helping out and being present.

The most important and unlikely role you may end up serving is a gushing faucet of hope. We do not know exactly what causes autism, but it has been strongly insinuated that genetics do not help as far as "preventing" autism. Therefore, any subsequent offspring in your gene pool run a risk of being diagnosed. Your role in this new chapter will be showing that your niece or nephew's life will be speckled with the same incremental improvements.

■ **Accept the unacceptable.** In a world where everything makes sense, your immediate loved ones accept you as part of their lives despite the inevitable Asperger's quirks. They will offer constructive criticism when it is deserved along with a modicum of sympathy. When you exhibit the leaps and bounds that are synonymous with the spectrum, they make an effort to exalt your self-worth to the stars. But it is not totally uncommon for families to have at least one relative who makes a decision to sever connections with all blood relations due to a reservoir of displaced anger. Or maybe they target a handful that annoy them or do not fit into their priorities. You could very well be part of that handful whose phone calls are not acknowledged. Facebook friendships are terminated or blocked as your own brother or sister treats you with the callousness of a high school acquaintance.

When a family member takes these draconian actions, they are often influenced by internal demons that expand beyond any ancient wrongdoings you have brought to the table. This is a tough situation. Give it time, be open to improvements, and try not to compound the negativity by being at the mercy of your sibling's choices.

■ **Give something back . . . damn it!** Like plenty of your peers, you may be advised to "let go" or forgive yourself. This is often easier said than done, which is why I recommend seeking out sibling support groups where you could serve as a guest speaker. It pierces my heart whenever I hear a neurotypical sibling tell me about how she resents the hatred her autistic brother has toward her. The hitting and outbursts are often a part of daily life, but it does not often come from hatred. In the majority of cases, it is merely a desperate attempt at communicating one's feelings. More understanding is needed. Siblings can play an enormous role in each other's success, and healing past wounds is well worth the effort.

ROMANTIC TRIALS

There have been numerous people of both neurotypical and Asperger's makeups who have made amazing contributions to humanity thanks to being relentless in their conquests. They pursued something even when most rational individuals would have moved on and accepted defeat. I may have mentioned earlier that Thomas Edison, who had autistic tendencies, made a thousand attempts to find the correct filaments that would nurse the artificial flame of the first lightbulb. And from what I have heard, the lightbulb he pioneered was more durable than the ones we are used to today. In some areas of life, persistence is a virtue. However, the same unremitting persistence that is credited for winning Nobel Prizes is not always practical when it comes to romantic pursuits. The transition to adulthood is the time to learn how to navigate this cumbersome path that is known to cause just as much anguish as ecstasy.

As you work on these skills, it's important to remember that you are intelligent, kindhearted, and deserving of the passion that sadly does not always reach us when we desire it. Unfortunately, those of us with Asperger's are at a big disadvantage when it comes to romance because it is typical for us to achieve romantic milestones in a belated fashion. We are making a valiant effort to catch up while experiencing such things like a first kiss or a first real relationship in our twenties. Or even later than that. Our first heartbreak may occur well into adulthood and create a level of heartache that prompts us to react like a typical fourteen-year-old because our romantic maturity may be at that level. We hold on just like we would with any other setback in hopes of restoring homeostasis. The consequences of not letting go in cases like this can be dire. We have rules that we impose upon ourselves, but society also has rules about this (in this way it is somewhat Asperger's-ish). The most important rule that we must learn before absorbing it the hard way is this:

Everyone has the right to be left alone if they choose this route after terminating a romance or declaring their lack of interest. It does not matter how abrupt or cruel the rejection may be, and nobody owes us anything.

Forget What You've Learned
in the Movies

Forget about every romantic comedy you have ever seen in which the male or female protagonist embarks on an unrelenting pursuit for their love interest. If you want some specific examples, how about *There's Something About Mary* or its sex change equivalent, *French Kiss*. The heroes of the movie go after what they want in the most inappropriate manner imaginable and have little concept of "letting go." The most flagrant example of rewarded "stalking" is probably *The Graduate*, in which Dustin Hoffman's character responds to advances from an aging seductress, pursues her daughter, follows the daughter to college, and makes the girl's special day all about him by ruining the wedding. In most of these films, they get what they want with the rare exception of *My Best Friend's Wedding*, which has a more realistic ending in which the wedding goes on as planned.

These are merely movies, however. Shadows of reality dancing in Plato's Cave in which life is skewed for our entertainment. They are not to be taken seriously, and the insanity of these characters must never be modeled for our own sake. An indefatigable pursuit of anyone, whether it is as a friend or romantic partner or anyone else, will often end with the pyrotechnics of disaster. The soft touch is a better strategy for anything in life, including romance.

We are a population that has trouble letting go, but it is now time to learn how to "let go" as fast as possible. In the world of romance, you either date for the rest of your lives, get married, or eventually the romance runs its inevitable course. Allow dating to be a festival of "letting go" and dismiss it as part of the process without thinking of it as a personal rejection. There will be plenty of false starts and failed attempts, but it's important to keep moving forward. If you cannot completely let go, then I plead with you to at least practice incremental "backing off." Unless an individual is obtaining a restraining order against you, contact someone only once in increments of six months at a time and send a gingerly worded email expressing your desire to maintain a friendship (even if you really want more). But hopefully you will come to realize your energy is better spent on those who will embrace your existence.

Years of disasters, disappointments, and consequences have helped me build up a library of skills that I hope will help you in your quest to find the happiness you deserve. Support groups are also wonderful opportunities to compensate for a lack of learning experiences.

■ **Consider romantic partners who are younger or older than you are.** The diagnostic criteria in the DSM-IV states that those on the autism spectrum are drawn to friends who are either younger or older, which is coldly described as "age-inappropriate friendships." In reality, there is nothing inappropriate about a union that delivers passion and happiness. We may mesh better with partners who are younger because our maturity, for the time being, may be closer to their chronological age. This is not an invitation to ask out every eighteen-year-old working at CVS, because like it or not . . . this can look somewhat creepy. And it is a *very* dangerous idea to pursue anyone (even if your intentions are initially platonic) who is under eighteen years of age since sexual relations between an adult and anyone under the age of eighteen is against the law. We also might find more success with partners who are older considering their priorities have evolved and will avoid judging us on trivial flaws in favor of the integrity and honesty that are the bedrock to any strong union. The first time someone shows you that you are worthy as more than a friend will accelerate hope in the greatest way possible.

■ **Use romance as a motivator to get your life in order.** Let's face the facts. If you have let yourself go and weigh three hundred pounds, you may not be viewed as so desirable. One of these days, it would be great if we could create an organization called "Carrot on a Stick" that would be an underground non-for-profit group designed to inspire those on the autism spectrum to make extremely positive life changes. If an individual loses one hundred pounds, then the company would reward him by assigning an exotic supermodel to hang out with him in public for a week and laud his positive qualities for the entire community to hear. The same service would be extended for Aspie women who could be trailed by Adonis gentlemen.

In case such a ridiculous fantasy never comes to fruition, small changes in lifestyle make a huge difference with tweaking the odds of success. People often want to associate with partners who strive to reach their ultimate potential.

■ **Avoid giving (or receiving) extravagant gifts and other grand gestures.** Over-the-top gestures of romance rarely work and will not enhance your chances of success. They also create pressure at the very beginning for the recipient and unnecessary anger if you are left stranded with an extra ticket to a Broadway show. First meetings should take place in modest settings. In other words, try Ruby Tuesday instead of the Gourmet Sushi Palace. Unsolicited gifts should come further into the relationship, but not from Day One. I have been on both sides of this phenomenon, and neither one feels right. Experiencing an occasional taste of my own medicine has created a greater sense of compassion and more awareness about the use of gifts. Don't go that route until you truly know where you stand and what you are both feeling.

■ **Steer clear from your coworkers.** Movie actors often have a rule: Never work with children or animals. Your rule should be to never attempt to date coworkers. Once in a while, an office romance blossoms, and the cosmic fragments lock into place. But there are those countless other times when it turns out to be an affront to one's dignity and/or a recipe for disaster. Pursuing those you work with is usually asking for trouble personally, professionally, and possibly even legally.

■ **Don't look overseas.** My advice with regard to initiating contact with people overseas is quite simple. *Do not* do it, or at least proceed with extreme caution. Out of the many millions of people here in the United States, there has to be at least one person who is compatible with your uniqueness. Just look a little harder as opposed to outsourcing your passion. The reason for this cynicism is that our population is infamous for being easy marks for Facebook spam promising an affair with photographs that look like they were cut-and-pasted from an online issue of *Vanity Fair*. Furthermore, I saw what my friends had to go through with their fortysomething-year-old uncle who lives with an undiagnosed case of Asperger's syndrome. His romance with a woman from the Dominican Republic ended in heartbreak when she promptly decided to leave after obtaining her green card.

■ **Disclose about having Asperger's syndrome.** Would you really want to be with someone who was not willing to sit down with you and hear about the labyrinth of your uniqueness? Three decades' worth of experiences have taught me that the truth comes out eventually, and the Asperger's subject must be addressed at the beginning. Any condition that will significantly affect any relationship should be acknowledged, in my opinion. This applies to Asperger's along with other ongoing challenges and conditions.

- **Understand what sexual harassment means.** By the time most of us reach our mid-twenties, we should understand the basics that will ward off the worst of trouble. The dictionary's definition of sexual harassment refers to the continued pursuit of someone who does not wish to be bothered. It is imposing yourself into the comfort zone of someone who has made it clear they are not interested in you and ignoring the concept of "no means no." Some of us have learned the hard way that there are also unwritten rules concealed beneath the literal rules in employee handbooks. In the workplace, sexual harassment or stalking is sadly defined as any type of romantic gesture that makes someone even slightly uncomfortable and prompts them to make a complaint to human resources. This gesture can be as innocent and short-lived as sending someone a bouquet of half a dozen red roses on Valentine's Day. Some employers will not bother to perform an investigation and will do what is easiest for them. It is a dangerous situation filled with room for misunderstandings and problems that are best avoided. Look elsewhere for romantic prospects to be on the safe side.

- **Educate yourself about maintaining healthy boundaries and reading nonverbal cues.** These are not easy topics and beyond the scope of this book to cover in full. However, they are essential areas to learn when entering the world of dating and relationships. Feelings and intentions are not always expressed through words. People don't always respond the way we want them to communicate. Nor do they always say what they mean. Sometimes we simply need to read the writing on the wall, accept that someone is "just not that into you," and move on. Vague replies, such as, "I'm extremely busy all of this month. I don't know . . . ," and someone's perpetual failure to answer their cell phone are telltale signs. These can be difficult lessons, but they are vital ones.

As you mature in this area, you will begin to look back on your past mistakes almost as if you're watching a tragicomic movie. You were obviously the starring actor, but the bumbling attempts and missed signals no longer resemble your experiences. For much of my young adult life, the pursuit seemed justified even after the woman insisted she just wanted to be friends or sever contact. Being ignored or rejected was an indication that I was not pushing hard enough to show that I deserved to be acknowledged. Rejection stung and created feelings of vulnerability. Fortunately, this has changed with compromise and modifications.

Learning to Take No for an Answer

As a high school senior, I had the opportunity to interview a ninth-grade girl named Blythe Auffarth, who was an actress on Nickelodeon and in movies. As part of the interview, which was for our high school newspaper, I asked her how she handles rejection.

Blythe answered with maturity beyond her fourteen years. "Rejection is mostly about 'type' in the acting business. You are rejected because you do not have the right hair, eye color, height, age, and many other things. I deal with rejection well and accept it as reality. Because most of the time . . . you will get rejected." Wise words that apply to all of us, not just Hollywood actors.

Most people will strike out a lot more times than celebrating a home run, which I learned while continuing with online dating. A person is sliced and diced into characteristics, such as body type, occupation, whether they have pets, whether they want children, or enjoy going out to nightclubs. One woman even rejected me because I admitted that I hated going to nightclubs and then she wrote in chat room shorthand, "U R weird." If you are someone with Asperger's who ventures into the world of online dating, one should have a sense of humor and embrace it as a Festival of Rejection or disastrous experiences. Not everyone is going to take it seriously or have consideration for your feelings. If you are someone with Asperger's syndrome who is tenacious with your goals and has an extremely difficult time "letting go," an exception must be made with romantic pursuits. The law is on the side of those who feel harassed and/or stalked. This was validated by a man sitting beside me at a Manhattan support group meeting who told us about his sentence in New York City's infamous Rikers

Island for violating a restraining order against a woman who occupied his every thought. His words should serve as a sobering warning for anyone unable to handle boundaries or rejections that will probably never be undone.

"I remember the day the judge sentenced me. I thought he would treat me as a kid who had made a mistake, but instead he treated me as a man and shipped me off to the darkest place I could go."

Part of moving forward is forgiving yourself for past transgressions. Perhaps you made the mistake out of ignorance or a lack of understanding. You've learned a valuable lesson. Don't make the learning curve steeper than it has to be. I ask that you learn from your mistakes, along with those made by me and anyone else who has already graduated from the School of Hard Knocks.

We must always understand that our greatest chances of success in romance rest with the same attitude we hopefully foster in a job situation or educational pursuits. It is critical to come to terms with the fact that we have something to offer for anyone who is willing to give us a fighting chance. The infrastructure for future success will be built on the mistakes you will make—and on the ones you avoid making in the first place.

THE COLLEGE EXPERIENCE

This may sound strange, but willingness and ability to make mistakes is vital. Then being able to reflect on these mistakes and strategize how to prevent further slipups in similar situations. This takes time and students often lack the patience or the ability to look at the larger picture to see that errors are teachers. Mistakes are the most important thing in learning. For many students, mistakes are not seen as opportunities to learn but rather opportunities to feel bad about themselves. Developing strong coping skills prior to coming to campus will certainly aid in the ability to sidestep a rough start.

—Stephen Motto, MS Ed., director of operations
for College and University Support Programs (CUSP)

S tarting college is a daunting step for most people, not just those who are living with Asperger's. This is true whether you will be living on campus or commuting each day for classes, and regardless of whether it's a four-year or two-year college, or a trade or vocational school.

Of course, our challenges with transitions and change can

be worse than others', which is why college requires extra preparation for most of us. Based on my college experience and those of many I have spoken with, it is fair to say that there will be some stumbles along the way. But if you're prepared and fortunate, these rough patches will amount to growing pains that you can weather, and the rewards will far outweigh the challenges. Without a doubt, earning a college degree is a major asset and accomplishment, and maybe just as important, the college experience is life-changing and world-expanding—one that pays rewards long after you move on to the next transition in your life.

Don't Expect Smooth Sailing Right Away

The first few weeks of college are rarely an accurate representation of your new life and the maturity required to succeed. Like a small child who is visiting Disney World, the first emotion you are likely to experience is raw euphoria that comes from the taste of freedom. You are free from the constant eye of parents and teachers. This can be both good and bad. Irresponsible decisions in college have consequences, but you probably won't feel their effects right away. As a child, it may have been difficult to get away with foolish decisions, especially if you had an Individualized Education Program (IEP) where it took a village to prevent failure. This means that as a college student you will have to make more of an effort to monitor your own actions. In some ways, college can serve as a sort of boot camp to help you transition into adulthood. The more you stay with the program, the faster you will see the desired results.

For a group of people who tend to flounder during transitional periods, college can be the Frankenstorm of sudden changes. We are ripped away from all sense of predictability and expected to metamorphose into independent adults overnight. This is a tall order even for neurotypical students, so give yourself time to adjust, without falling into bad habits that will take more effort to undo.

The first weeks of college do not represent reality and can seem like a Veritable Cornucopia of Pleasures. This is the first time nobody will order you when to go to bed. Or when it is time to cease abusing the snooze alarm and get ready for class. You have unconditional access to beverages that infuse artificial energy, and the nighttime becomes an untapped reservoir of time. It became possible for me to procrastinate and waste an entire day only to compensate by staying up all night long. My nighttime work competed with Archie Bunker's bigoted commentary and old episodes of *The Facts of Life*. Most nights very little work was completed despite staying up until three in the morning. I learned a hard lesson that the more unstructured time one has at their disposal, the more time may be squandered. Use it wisely. Here are a few tips you might find helpful:

■ **Limit distractions.** My freshman year commenced back in 2000 when the Internet was fairly new and resembled a Rube Goldberg contraption compared to what we have these days. There was no social media like Twitter, and Mark Zuckerberg was still a high school student. Our social networking was limited to America Online instant messages and bland profiles that contained only basic information. YouTube did not exist with its millions of time-gobbling videos that can take over your attention for hours on end. Today's Internet offerings up the ante considerably, presenting many more ways to waste time.

Like alcohol, marijuana, or other drugs, social media and on-demand entertainment like YouTube and streaming movies and TV can be a dangerous distraction. Most of us, in order to justify bad habits, make up justifications that do not make sense. Dabbling in the Internet while performing assignments is rarely conducive to efficient studying even though we have the "Whistling While We Work Theory." It is impossible to complete a close reading of Shakespeare's *Hamlet* while also engaged in a video with kittens meowing along to a Justin Bieber song. The wisest thing to do is turn the laptop on Airplane Mode whenever you are in Studying Mode. The Airplane Mode feature on all modern laptops is a well-kept secret that will block Facebook and its unrelenting parade of mundane news. (And anything else Internet-related that will clash with the task at hand.)

The study skills that will be formed with your own grit and determination are going to be the first part of the battle. When you have cleared this hurdle, you will be ready to take on anything that comes next.

■ **Get off on the right foot with your roommate(s).** I've heard it said that the roommate selection process can seem like a twisted conspiracy because for some reason many students seem to be paired up with radically dissimilar personalities and preferences. (Perhaps there are hidden cameras streaming a reality show built on constant conflict, like a real-life version of Neil Simon's classic *The Odd Couple*.) Ending up in one of these odd pairings can certainly make your transition more difficult. Living with the same person for a whole school year is not easy, and even if you and your roommate are a great match, there will be moments where you step on each other's toes. But the worst damage will come from letting problems fester instead of bringing them to the table early on. Therefore, I believe it is prudent to disclose that you have Asperger's syndrome to your new roommate and explain what your main challenges are. If possible, come up with some suggestions for ways to avoid foreseeable problems and make your daily routine together run smoothly. Some of the horror stories I've heard include someone who accidentally locked out his neurotypical roommate as he was stranded outside in a bath towel. Then he refused to return and unlock the door out of fear of being late to class. There is also a time to give up even if we do not believe in "letting go." When your roommate issues start interfering with your education, then it may be time to appeal to your college's residential office to look into the possibility of a replacement.

■ **Put high school on a back burner.** Toward the end of the series, the adult narrator of *The Wonder Years* lamented, "Change is never easy. You fight to hold on. You fight to let go." There is a natural temptation to resurrect old routines or attempt to reconnect with high school friends, acquaintances, or teachers. This desire is a product of human evolution; we are attracted to environments that offer us predictability, familiarity, and comfort in order to avoid unforeseen danger and increase our chances of survival. But we are no longer living in the tundra, and those of us with Asperger's sometimes cling to our old creature comforts in ways that are not always appropriate—or in our best interests. One of my younger peers was reprimanded for sneaking back onto the high school bus in a pilgrimage to this edifice of nostalgia. If you are going to reconnect with old teachers, it is critical to do so in careful moderation because your former mentors have their hands full with the students they are currently teaching. You might visit your old haunts once in a while, but it will not take long before tolerance is chipped away like the candy shell of an M&M. If you cannot handle letting go completely, then try compromising with only one visit per semester during school hours. Any subsequent visits should be connected with public events such as fairs, plays, and sporting events. Letting go of the past is hard, but it is a part of the college experience, and it often leads to growth and new discoveries.

Of course, you might maintain some close friendships from high school or earlier. These can be great bonds, even lifelong ones. However, I believe that 90 percent of your energy should be spent supplementing your success in the college environment. As you push forward into the adult world, you will continue to find that many relationships are built out of convenience, and the pruning of unnecessary friendships is very common in the neurotypical population. (It may also take place in your life when priorities change and you start taking on more responsibilities.) When we depend on past connections as a substitute for what is temporarily lacking in college, we set ourselves up for disappointment. Like any other temporary fix, it does not address the real challenge at hand, which is making new friends and finding a way to live more fully in the present.

■ **Redefine your attitudes about grades—both good and bad ones.** Report cards may have taken on a sinister nature during your adolescence and high school years. The consequence of earning a C-minus on your report card might have been the source of unrelenting haranguing from parents who worried about your future or even viewed a nonstellar academic performance as a reflection on themselves. Unless your main goal is to earn one of the coveted seats in Harvard Medical School, the essence of what you learn and your incremental improvements will be the true barometer of success. A former William Smith dean named Amy Teel said it best when she told a group of us:

> *There should never be any student who leaves Hobart and William Smith Colleges with a 4.0 GPA even though a handful of students do every year. If you leave with this GPA, then we have failed you. And worst of all, you have not done enough to challenge yourself.*

For some of you, academic accolades may have served as the lone buoy for your self-esteem during periods of social isolation. With that said, it is time to embrace more challenges and know you have something more to offer than stellar grades. As a college student, you will encounter at least one subject that is insurmountable. This may be a new experience for you, especially if you made it through high school with only a moderate amount of studying. You will drag yourself across the finish line with your ragged fingernails, but your grade will not be a reflection of your tenacity. The true lessons of college include learning how to face these challenges and do your best.

Fitting in Without Hiding
Who You Really Are

Revealing that you have Asperger's is never an easy task, but the benefits are almost always worth the risk. Attempting to fit into the student body like a camouflaged tree sloth is exhausting and eventually pointless. Dealing with the occasional misunderstandings is even worse. Think of yourself as a brand-new car with its lights on and no ignition charging up the battery. You will be able to last for a long time by hiding who you are, but will eventually burn out. Consult your parents, other trusted members of your support system, and the college counseling department to explore how best to disclose your diagnosis.

When I look back on my collegiate would-haves, should-haves, and could-haves, there is always the same persistent fantasy: disclosing my Asperger's early on, to explain some of my more erratic behavior. My pastime of sprinting all over campus for no reason earned me the moniker of "Running Jesse" followed by more cruel nicknames such as "Sketchy and Scary Jesse." When I finally did reveal the diagnosis in the middle of my college career and stopped running, it was amazing how quickly public opinion changed for the better. It did not, however, reverse some of the social damage that could have been prevented in the first place. While students on campus may display ignorance, they have a greater capacity to absorb education when we make it accessible.

- **Check to see what fork everyone else is using.** In general, it is best to model the behavior of your fellow students in the classroom environment. In high school, your class clowning may have been tolerated in moderation. But if you have noticed that nobody else has made a wisecrack for the first three weeks of college, it would be in your best interest to not break the ice as the self-proclaimed College Harlequin.

Some of the unwritten rules of social etiquette might seem silly, but it's not our job to rewrite them, and attempting to do so will only set you apart (not in a good way). When we struggle to master table manners, we must learn the basics even though some of it makes no sense. We are told to wait until everyone at the table has been served before we start eating. (Personally, I would not care if someone began eating before my food showed up!) For some reason, the soup spoon must always be gently placed at the side of my plate instead of inside the soup bowl. But table manners become more cumbersome when there are invisible rules beneath rules. At some dining tables, you will look foolish if you sit with your food growing cold when you can simply look around to see that everyone else has already started eating.

Address Problems Early On

If you do struggle or experience failure, do not simply give up. Accept reality and take action to improve your situation.

■ **Find a tutor the moment you begin to struggle.** This will be the only time in your life when this service is free of charge, and it is not a sign of weakness to seek some help. Most tutors are veterans of the same classes and may give you tips on how to study or what is expected by the professor.

■ **Find a new spot for studying.** Studying alone in your room can become an isolating experience, so it is worth making trips to the library. Regardless of our awkwardness and discomfort around new people, we are still social beings and will flourish around other souls simultaneously striving for academic success. Experiment with different settings (noise levels, number of people around, and so on). To make the process a little more bearable, I would study in the library basement where the archives were housed behind a cage-like fence. It was fun to pretend that a friendly and intelligent monster slept there during the day, only to be released by the library caretakers upon nightfall to read literature and not disturb students with its hideous appearance.

■ **Don't compound your problems with shame and anger.** You may be placed on "academic probation" if you have a disastrous first semester. It is a friendly warning that if you do not show some significant improvement, then you could be asked to leave campus. This may feel like someone has super-glued a dunce cap to your head, but it is actually a chance to rise to the occasion. Most of us become stronger when we falter as opposed to experiencing the fleeting exhilaration of winning. This is one area where some demons of Asperger's can actually double as a strength, like in the second *Terminator* movie when Arnold Schwarzenegger returns as a benevolent savior instead of a mechanical murderer. College should be a chance to stop thinking of failure as the boogeyman and more like a catalyst for consistent success.

Always remember that you are in extremely good company if you have an academic setback.

- Steven Spielberg was rejected by his dream school, the University of Southern California School of Cinematic Arts, three times.

- Walt Disney was fired by a newspaper editor for lacking innovation and vision. His subsequent businesses failed before the 1938 premiere of *Snow White and the Seven Dwarfs* finally turned things around.

- Albert Einstein (who many speculate had Asperger's) did not speak until four years old or start reading until age seven. His teachers insisted that he would never amount to anything. As a young adult, he worked as a lowly assistant in the Swiss Patent Office.

■ **Create the "half-caf" of academia.** This is the ultimate win-win situation when wading into one of the most volatile transitions of your life. One of the most common complaints for any college student is how their classes are either too difficult or too easy. At Starbucks, there is a compromise for those who cannot handle a lot of caffeine, but still need a stimulant to launch the day. The baristas give you a cup mixed with half-decaf and half-regular coffee. Your first semester should be spent taking two classes that offer a moderate challenge (like Intro to Sociology) and two classes that are not academically rigorous (such as the Magic of Ornithology).

■ **Early is on time, on time is late, and late is never . . .** This particular phrase will be your salvation, especially considering many college professors are not going to be so lenient when you consistently turn in material late due to procrastination or focusing on nonpriorities. The ideal scenario is to have a fake deadline, and the real deadline will serve as a grace period. There is also a real possibility that your printer will break down twenty minutes before class after riding a nightlong wave of artificial energy fueled by a diet of Red Bulls and barely diluted grains of instant coffee. Turning in material early on a habitual basis will earn you a stellar reputation that will increase the chances of receiving a "break" when something is handed in late due to events beyond your control.

■ **Make your arguments in a respectful fashion.** Some professors are naturally stingy about giving out A's for great work and will become offended if you express your disgust. It often amounts to a hill of beans anyway if you, God forbid, receive a B. But if grades are that important to you, then go see your professor during office hours, instead of belligerently saying, "I deserve a better grade."

■ **The increments always win.** Fans of the macabre have lived in awe of Stephen King and how he can crank out at least fifty bestselling novels over the course of his lifetime. Until I read his memoir, *On Writing*, I always assumed he was a demented figure who typed his creations with fingers possessed by the devil. But this theory turned out to be erroneous because Stephen King only writes two thousand words a day—a *pathetic* four pages in Microsoft Word. When we do the math, this amounts to a one-hundred-eighty-thousand-word novel in just three months! While everyone with Asperger's is different, we tend to straddle the extremes of taking on too much at once or not getting started because the task seems too immense. There is nothing shameful about being somewhat pathetic while starting any of your intimidating assignments because being *consistently* pathetic over an extended period of time will amount to a huge accomplishment!

More Strategies for Success

■ **Practice becoming your own advocate.** For the first time in your education, your parents will not be in continuous communication with your teachers. You may be entitled to some basic accommodations like extra time on tests and use of a laptop during final exams if you also suffer from dysgraphia (poor handwriting). My family chose Hobart because of the special education services that were available, and this made a profound difference. But no matter what, it will be up to you to advocate for services needed to become successful. The Academic Support Center was kind enough to deliver a letter to every professor about my Asperger's syndrome, but it may be a good idea to write your own letter stating that you will accept feedback if there are problems and will do what you can to be successful. Because they knew about my disability, most professors were tolerant toward my eccentricities and rarely overreacted over the occasional stunt like skating into class on in-line skates on my birthday! A couple of times, I was also late turning in a paper and walked through the city of Geneva, New York, to hand it in at the professor's private residence. Keep in mind that not all professors are going to appreciate these flamboyant gestures, and it is critical to adjust your routine when necessary.

■ **Find your tribe.** Chances are good there will be other students who are also coping with Asperger's or relatable challenges. By reaching out to them, you can tap into a great resource, one you can each draw strength from as you find your way through the college experience. One student I came to know became this type of inspiration for me. She was two years ahead of me, and she succeeded in double dipping into trouble shortly after starting her freshman year with a subpar

GPA along with other shenanigans that required disciplinary action. For students at many other institutions, this might have meant expulsion. Fortunately, Hobart and William Smith was a more benevolent college than some. Alisa's grades improved at the steady pace of an inebriated tortoise . . . but she fought her way back from the precipice of academic failure. She also found a niche on campus where students were more tolerant toward her lapses in social graces. With the support of accepting friends and classmates, she discovered success, social acceptance, and even graduated on time.

■ **Take a mini-vacation from campus when necessary.** You will be almost constantly around other people, which can become overwhelming for even the most gregarious neurotypical individuals. You are even sharing your bedroom with someone else. Sometimes it may be necessary to take a night off to go to a cheap motel in close proximity from the campus or return home for a weekend if it is practical.

■ **Decide to consume alcohol in strict moderation or not at all.** Peer pressure may come from a fear that everyone else is having fun and you are missing out on the din of this alcohol-saturated celebration. We have also dubbed alcohol as "social skills in a bottle" under the fallacy that it melts away awkwardness and allows us to infiltrate any group. In reality, excessive alcohol consumption is a form of masochism and you will end up impressing nobody. Morning comes as it always does, and you will experience a self-inflicted sickness unlike any other. If you insist on learning this lesson the hard way, then remember that sensation of waking up with the universe spinning around in a kaleidoscope of extreme nausea. Alcohol and other negative influences will be the last thing that culminates in social success.

■ **Do something benevolent with your downtime.** You will probably take four classes a semester that meet for fifty-five minutes three days a week or at least an hour and a half two days a week. The rest of the time is for studying or activities of your choosing. There are innumerable opportunities to get involved with extracurricular activities that will allow your classmates to experience the real *you*. Habitat for Humanity and even teaching reading skills to disadvantaged youths will give you a sense of purpose and create advocates on campus. Most colleges sponsor events like a "Day of Service," which give students the chance to make contributions to the community. You might discover an untapped interest or skill and meet potential friends, too.

One of my greatest college memories took place years later when I returned as an alumnus to give a speech about Asperger's syndrome. A large gathering of students with social difficulties took place at a dean's house. I was struck by the fact that unlike me at the very beginning of my college experience, these students seemed to be happy and believed they had a purpose. Some of the students were making a contribution by assisting professors with projects. Others carved out a reputation in clubs where their neurotypical classmates were exposed to common characteristics of honesty and reliability. Furthermore, any acceptance that was temporarily withheld from the neurotypical population on campus would germinate from this powerful group that did not exist ten years ago. There were smiles, and the night was lacking in tearful war stories. This experience was a powerful reminder that those of us with Asperger's can thrive in the college environment with a little support—and that any campus will not be as strong without our contributions.

TIME MANAGEMENT, ORGANIZATION, AND NOT LETTING GO!

Recently I visited Pier 1 for the first time and was intrigued by the store's carnival-like atmosphere of trinkets and treasures. There was one section in particular that seemed to be catered to the autism community. It was a rotating mini-rotunda of magnetic beads, paddleballs, cup-and-ball toys, wind-up figurines, and other knickknacks. I especially liked the magnetic beads that took the shape of tiny torpedoes and made a hissing, rattlesnake noise upon connecting in midair. Then my attention turned to the sleek, water-filled cylinder capped with circular buttresses for support on any desktop. Upon closer examination, I realized it was a tool of time management entombed with a tiny hourglass containing enough crimson talc powder for five minutes. It was titillating how flipping it over caused the primitive clock to propel to the top . . . buoyed by an eternal air bubble. I purchased the ten-dollar novelty item with the false hope that it would help me with the continuous crisis of poor time management and procrastination.

Becoming an adult means coming to face our deficiencies in executive functioning skills. Plenty of us lack that internal diatribe that pushes us to "just get going already." You have a free day so perhaps this would be the right time to de-clutter the bedroom instead of putting it off for months on end (or more). Your dentist appointment begins at 10:00 a.m. It is now 9:04 a.m., so why haven't you bothered to start showering and brushing your teeth? What about traffic and other uncontrollable factors that might interfere with the approximate travel time?

We are bombarded by plenty of distractions and time wasters. In my experience, the most infamous of this stimulation would be Netflix streaming. Some of us have already been seduced by the gushing self-gratification of hundreds of hours' worth of classic television shows that had been off the air for years. I found myself wasting entire days and nights catching up on cartoon reruns of *Inspector Gadget* and soaking up *The Wonder Years* with Fred Savage. There are too many ways to piss away the day, week, month, or even one's entire life with an endless variety of stimulation. Netflix, YouTube, *Angry Birds*, Facebook, Twitter, and the like should not be referred to as time wasters. It is much more appropriate to describe them as piranhas of productivity.

In reality, we feel impotent, and there is very little that can completely liberate us from the tendencies that compel us to waste time and put things off until the last minute. We can purchase massive desktop calendars, colorful Post-it notes, and unique alarm clocks. Online I found an alarm clock molded into the shape of a *Space Invaders* arcade game that is programmed to play gaming tunes from my early childhood. Perhaps the virtual jingles could churn nostalgia into a form of caffeine and rouse me out of bed at an extremely early hour. Then my waking hours would be exploited to the fullest, like an expired antelope whose skeletal remains were picked clean by every beast in the African wilderness. Sometimes I equate procrastination to a hard-partying binge drinker who spends Saturday morning with his face in the commode before staggering back to bed with the universe spinning like a merry-go-round from hell. He does not understand the rationale for such self-inflicted torture or why he did not learn his lesson from the last experience. And the night two weeks before that. But he once again makes an empty promise that this morning will never have an encore. Albert Einstein once defined insanity as, "Doing the same thing over and over again and expecting different results." Therefore, we can conjecture that the behaviors leading to disasters in time management and organization certainly qualify.

Along with the arcade game replica, there should be alarm clocks that appeal to various sectors of mankind. In the future, there will be more complex alarm clocks that rouse people out of bed with the aid of dancing holograms similar to the ones found in the Haunted Mansion of Disney World's Magic Kingdom. The first of these inventions would cater to the most affluent, but as the technology becomes more outdated, they disperse among the rest of us.

For the perpetually single and involuntarily celibate man (like me, for instance), there would be holograms of dancing *Playboy* bunnies with sultry voices whispering about pancake banquets and circular ham garnished with poached eggs waiting downstairs.

"All you have to do is step out of bed and come downstairs. I will be waiting. Get us while we are hot, baby!"

As the snooze alarm is abused, the sultry voice will turn incrementally more shrill and demanding. The same options will be available for the women with romantic lives as desolate as Patty and Selma Bouvier from *The Simpsons*. Adonis holograms will rouse women out of bed, too. Furthermore, a healthy percentage of proceeds from this invention would be donated to autism programs. A win-win for all.

Until these inventions burst onto the novelty market, I use a few basic tactics to help myself stay on track. For example, the alarm on my phone is usually set a day in advance and detonates in increments of fifteen minutes apart. I am now conditioned to listen to that sound and understand that the alarm's shrieking is an indication that something is on my schedule around that time. *Think, Jesse. What do you have to do that you are obviously forgetting?*

In addition, my keys and other important items are never

tossed around haphazardly. Rather, they are always placed in one of two designated homing stations. But the most important change I've made is leaving myself extra time—lots of it.

Dialing Down the Stress

And if we look back, we may come to realize that many of our negative Asperger's characteristics have been exacerbated during times of intense pressure. Some of it was beyond our control, but many other instances have been self-inflicted. Whether we have Asperger's or not, everyone has experienced that sinister feeling that the world is closing in on us, either from a looming project deadline or from waiting until the last second to get ready for a job interview. Aside from worrying about filtering raunchy jokes or telling incriminating stories, you may find yourself desperately searching for your tie that has disappeared. It is not crumpled on the bathroom floor, languishing at the bottom of the laundry hamper, and may have very well slipped into the crevices of the couch leading to Narnia. You eventually find the tie but are now frantically tearing the house apart looking for the car keys. There is simmering rage because the fates have conspired to ruin another opportunity as family members offer criticism for being disorganized. Ridiculous clichés rebound like verbal Ping-Pong balls, such as "Where was the last place you saw it?" (This is perhaps the most despised, nonconstructive phrase behind

"Others have it much worse" and "Just let it go . . . move on already.") If these mornings and similar catastrophes of lapsed time are a regular occurrence, then the advice in this chapter will help you avoid these unforced errors in the future. I hope that, like me, you will have a moment of epiphany, realizing that so many of these mornings could have been easily prevented by waking up earlier in the morning. Or even preparing a little the night before.

I've come to see the humor in some of my pressure-filled, running-late debacles. In haste, I have set my car's GPS wrong and ended up at the wrong address and even the wrong town. I once ended up going to John Jay High School in Hopewell Junction, New York, instead of the John Jay High School in Westchester. These gaffes kept people waiting and took a toll on my psyche. They are mistakes I am careful not to make again.

As a college senior, I attended an orientation for a yearlong honors project, where a dean explained that no extension has or ever will be given in this program. He told us:

> *It does not matter if the project is due at 10:00 a.m. and you learn that your father just died at 9:50 a.m. I am down on my knees begging you to hand in your honors papers early just in case something happens. And if you wait until the last second to print it out, then I promise you that the printer is going to jam. It always does. You will ask yourselves, "Why now?" But these problems always happen because even technology will sense your distress!*

This was great advice that has helped me focus on preparation and organization. Here are a few strategies to try:

- **Develop a nightly ritual.** This will help you ensure a sane morning and reduce stress. Your glasses, wallet, train ticket, and anything else needed for the next day should be lined on a counter like toy soldiers.

- **Identify your black holes.** What are the most common places that your lost items are usually found? These might be under the couch cushions, concealed by a newspaper in the place where you thought you last saw it, or in the pocket of your pants crumpled on the bathroom floor. Try to be more careful when you're in those parts of your home. Don't leave important items there out of habit.

- **Get a calendar.** Purchase one of those massive desktop calendars that covers a large portion of your work area and serves as a blotter. It can function as a veritable bible of timekeeping. If you prefer a different style of calendar, that's fine—but make sure it's one that you will actually use.

- **Write it down.** Immediately write down your new commitments on your calendar. I find it helpful to text new commitments to myself seconds after hearing them and remember to transfer them on the calendar later that evening. Your skills may have been stunted by well-meaning parents, teachers, and friends who over-reminded you and tried to take care of the details for you. It is never too late to develop your own memory, which cannot function without writing down commitments and tasks.

■ **Choose your special interests wisely.** There is nothing wrong with hobbies, regardless of how unusual or age-inappropriate, as long as you are not hurting anyone (including yourself) or doing anything illegal. You should be proud of your passion for collecting *Teenage Mutant Ninja Turtles* memorabilia from the 1980s. Or maybe you revel in exploring country roads on Sunday evenings to photograph birds in the wild. I still go trick-or-treating and stay up past midnight on October 30th to carve jack-o'-lanterns. But some special interests will monopolize much of your time and energy needed to function in the adult world. The first week of my winter vacations were spent writing monotonous Christmas cards to friends and acquaintances in college. At this stage in adulthood, it is not practical to sacrifice so much time to these nonsensical pursuits. Any special interest that usurps more than a solid day of your time each week and is not conducive to more adult goals is probably worth placing limitations on or even eliminating completely.

■ **Celebrate the most banal of your accomplishments.** Reading the statuses on Facebook will drive you crazy when people flaunt their job promotions, engagements, wedding plans, and the arrival of their cherubic babies. Everyone seems happy and is seizing the day, unlike yourself. One of the best ways to generate pride is through celebrating the smallest achievements that were put off yesterday. Even your most shameful days of laziness may yield accomplishments. Some days will be tackled with the passion of an ergonomics efficiency expert, and other days will produce a bag of decomposing weeds because the only thing you accomplished that day was one hour of lawn care.

■ **Get up earlier.** Liberate yourself from the cocoon of your comfortable bed before 8:00 a.m. to ensure a productive day. Also complete the bulk of mindless chores (dishwashing, taking out the garbage, laundry) in the early morning. The psychological caffeine may come in the form of a morning routine and propels your Asperger's gears into motion. We often do much better with set routines and can use this to our advantage.

■ **Make mini-goals.** Breaking down a mammoth task into tiny increments is the only way to tackle it.

■ **Remember that the tortoise always wins.** This was the best advice offered at the start of my 2,174-mile-long Appalachian Trail hike at the start of 2005. My fellow hikers told me to move like a sloth and focus on only completing eight to fifteen miles a day. And there would be some sections so inundated with obstacles that even the pace of one mile per hour would be impressive. Do not be hard on yourself, especially if progress continues to be made. Some of us with Asperger's tend to take on too much at once, with the best of intentions, and it almost always leads to getting little accomplished. (If you need a proper analogy to go with this description, think of Lucy and Ethel trying to sort chocolates on the assembly line in that classic episode of *I Love Lucy*.)

■ **Keep an activity journal.** Try writing down everything you do for a twenty-four-hour period. You will see where the time goes and identify habits that are sucking up your time. I tried this once, and it was eye-opening. Some of the things on my list were:

- Spent ten minutes washing out every empty food container. (There is a fear they would be rejected by the recycling company because of residue, and I also salvaged toilet paper rolls from the trash can that were entangled in a web of used dental floss.)

- Handwrote a few three-page-long Christmas cards to obscure acquaintances to avoid taking on more pressing responsibilities.

- Nursed a cup of scalding hot coffee for twenty minutes while watching the episode of *SpongeBob SquarePants* where Mr. Krabs and Plankton magically switch lives to prove the grass is not always greener on the other side.

- Flapped my hands and spoke gibberish in front of Jimmy the cat's perplexed face. Gimleshka . . . foloshiash . . . scotchguard . . . sketchmeister.

- Filled idle time with repressed memories followed by fits of rage.

■ **Stay busy to stay sane.** Remember that being busy and active can help keep negative thoughts at bay. Think back to your childhood during periods when you were aimless. Odds may be strong that the words "I am bored" were immediately followed by trouble. This trend continued into my early adulthood when idle time was filled with bad habits or ridiculous pranks.

It may not be possible to let go of anger or obsessive thoughts entirely, but it is your choice to let this ancient arsenic ruin what could have been a productive day. Negative energy may be close to the surface, but focusing on the constructive activities that you want and need to do should help you expel these toxins, at least in the short term.

■ **Realize you're not alone.** It is critical to understand that difficulties in time management are not just an Asperger's crisis, even though our condition may be exacerbating the problem. Wasted and unbudgeted time is an epidemic in our culture, which is rife with distractions. Don't let them sabotage your goals. Don't confuse instant gratification for the genuine satisfaction of accomplished goals and real achievements.

■ **Make Asperger's your ally.** Having Asperger's has also gifted us with the ability to find creative ways to escape unhealthy situations and incorporate obsessions into solving other problems. An aversion to exercise was resolved by using YouTube as a motivator when I walked the treadmill while playing intros for 1990s sitcoms on the Android phone. A laser-like focus can be directed at our To-Do List. Invent a game to make productivity more fun. Chase those mini-thrills all day long until you've won the game (and the battle against procrastination).

We should all do ourselves a huge favor and stop attaching our difficulties with executive functioning to innate character defects and unflattering descriptions that have siphoned our self-esteem in the past. *You are lazy, unmotivated, stupid . . . wasting your life . . . why can't you learn from your mistakes and grow up?* It is better to think of issues with organization and time management like any other skill that will grow stronger with effort and persistence. The day will come when you finally *get it*, and who you used to be will merely serve as a haunting reminder of how important it is to maintain momentum. Your inability to let go and other deficiencies that may have contributed to the problem should also serve to help liberate you. Start today.

BEATING A GAMING ADDICTION

At times when my self-worth plummets, I find myself reflecting back upon my time playing the game with the deepest nostalgia. I had created and connected myself with this persona that became a part of my identity. I had much to offer in the gaming world to my peers online, and this gave me a sense of worth and purpose. I was so invested in the game that my only clear memories are of things I was doing in it at the time, people I was with, and the euphoric thrill it was. I was so lost in the game I practically lived there. It was conceived at one point that I may never live independently, drive a car, or pursue a higher education. I am doing all three and much more now and through years of work have I established myself at this point. Feeling worthy and knowing I have much to offer are powerful tools at my disposal to fight back any regression in my progress.

—Joshua Adams

Addictions have been known to plague humanity, in a variety of forms, for centuries. They tend to latch onto the coattails of our vulnerabilities and deep-seated demons. Falling under the spell of drugs, alcohol, gambling, and other addictions is nothing new. But what is relatively new is the slippery slope of seeking respite from reality on the Internet, particularly in the form of online gaming.

Everyone—whether they have Asperger's or not—feels the need to escape reality from time to time. For those of us with Asperger's, fantastical worlds like Never-Never Land and the rest of the Disney universe offered a much needed escape from the routine of not fitting in, feeling misunderstood, and other daily challenges. As we enter adolescence and young adulthood, too many of us begin to turn to online gaming to provide a convenient escape—an alternate world where we are accepted, successful, and most of all . . . understood.

There is nothing wrong with enjoying online games. I'm old enough to recall playing the classic 1980s arcade games *Donkey Kong* and *Pac-Man*—low-tech machines that offered me the opportunity to do something I couldn't do in real life: wreak revenge on the bullies and various other "bad guys" in order to restore justice and order, if only for a brief moment.

I think the addictive nature of arcade games from my early 1980s childhood came from the impossibility of winning. The levels grew harder and harder until the player eventually perished. In that sense, the games were similar to life, except there is a chance to always start over. The games were not an activity devoid of lessons, however. They taught me to never become complacent or rest on my laurels, to keep fighting for a few more minutes of playing time, and continue feeding that ambition to move to the next level.

My parents wisely banned home entertainment systems during most of my childhood. They worried that I would play all the time and would be unable to stop. Finally, they broke down and purchased a Super Nintendo as a reward for good behavior in fifth grade. Unlike neurotypical children, I could not garner self-esteem through sports or by building social relationships with peers. Therefore, they tolerated something that always put a smile on my face.

Speaking Our Language

The same Joker-like smile that I had playing Super Nintendo resonates through much of the autism population. I am convinced that many video game designers either have Asperger's or something else that sets them apart from the neurotypical world. They were probably short-changed as far as athletic ability and social graces. Many of the virtual characters that are cherished by popular culture are inadvertent representations of these inferiority complexes. Mario, for instance, is the ultimate poster child for self-delusion and the insatiable need to prove one's self against larger foes. He got screwed as far as stature (and probably anatomy, if stereotypes of vertically-challenged, overcompensating men have any validity). Furthermore, he is matched up against an enormous gorilla that has an eye for petite women. Mario's perpetual rescues earn him a cartoon heart that makes him a hero, leveling out the unevenness of characters who are freakishly dissimilar.

I'm sure the game makers don't set out to cause harm in the form of addiction and a loss of productivity. I doubt that anyone could create something so beautiful and engrossing if their heart was not in the right place. They envision and create a universe where the weak and emasculated can feel like winners. Kids with poor physical coordination could become gods of the basketball court and outperform neurotypical youths in this magical dimension.

New Games for a New Age

The main reason I was not seized by video game addiction as a child is that I was the last generation to play outside until the streetlights signaled it was time to come home for dinner. The majority of the two-dimensional games were mediocre, and our attention span was very short. We eventually beat the games or the luster wore off like a cheap varnish. I would plead with my parents to buy me new cartridges, and they would sometimes comply. But the thrill was not there.

In contrast, today's online games are far more varied, realistic, and readily available.

FarmVille, *CityVille*, and *Mafia Wars* hold no appeal for me (in fact, I can't stand the relentless invitations for them on Facebook, which need to be constantly swatted away like houseflies). But they hold great appeal to many—so much so that some individuals come to believe that it is normal to spend hours tending to virtual crops. (There are probably some real agrarians who do not spend *that* much energy on their livelihood, I would bet.)

Gerry was a victim of *FarmVille* who seemed to have everything going for him, or at least this was my first impression when I caught up with him ten years after high school. He had married Vanessa, who was one of the school beauty queens. They had both stayed in good shape and were pursuing career paths of their choice. But the day came when Gerry suffered a traumatic brain injury at his worksite. While on disability leave, Gerry was sucked into the all-consuming world of *FarmVille*. He played it all hours of the day and night until finally coming to the conclusion that he was never going to stop. Drastic times called for extreme measures, and Gerry finally unhooked the entire computer and dragged it out into the yard. Eventually the rain came and drowned all circuits.

I asked Gerry what drew him into the game—a game that has always seemed unappealing to me.

"It is always there," he replied without missing a beat. "All I had to do is turn on the computer, and it was always there." At that moment, I understood.

The Internet has combined addictive gaming with a faux sense of community. For some individuals who are severely challenged by Asperger's, this might be their first foray into maintaining social relationships. *World of Warcraft* is probably the most infamous massively multiplayer online role-playing game (MMORPG), with characters that grow stronger while accumulating wealth that is gold in this medieval nether-world, but worthless in the authentic universe. A male friend of mine simply referred to it as "The Game." His girlfriend in the game was a gorgeous blonde with supernatural beauty. Along with his family, we helped him recognize the signs that the player behind this pubescent goddess was actually a man with a fraudulent profile photo. And the only thing holding this "relationship" together was my friend handing over his gold earned by vanquishing a series of mythological creatures. Yes, that is yet another danger of such games. They are a petri dish for scams and bullying. Players are pitted into a codependent relationship with other gamers. Not even death ends the characters' hold on the player. In some cases, if they have banked enough currency, they can merely "buy their way out of death."

A female friend with Asperger's shared with me her Sims universe that allowed her to create a sprawling house complete with a swimming pool, man cave, gushing fountain, and amenities that rival those of A-list movie stars. The latest crisis she is dealing with happens to be a meddling social service officer who is visiting the mansion to check on the triplets that she is struggling to take care of all by herself. Against my will, she recently made me one of the characters, and apparently I am now pregnant thanks to an intimate encounter with an alien. Don't let this happen to you!

Getting Help

While online games may be a harmless hobby for some, they can pose a serious risk for many people, including those of us on the spectrum. If you seem to be developing an addiction to gaming, it does not mean that you are weak, a loser, or immature. Seek the help of a qualified professional. In some cases, an intervention can be effective, presented with the appropriate dosage of tough love and sympathy, preferably with the help of a professional, who can also help design a plan for long-term recovery. And even if you have not experienced this addiction, you can provide support for those in the throes of its grasp.

Here are a few warning signs to look for if you're concerned that you might have a gaming addiction:

- You have neglected such "time wasters" as personal hygiene rituals in favor of gaming.

- Your version of "midnight" occurs at six o'clock in the morning, and the new day of gaming begins at four in the afternoon. There is little concept of time, holidays, or weekends.

- Your physique has suffered due to time spent playing the game. Most of your energy comes from caffeine and energy beverages.

- Whatever friendships you have maintained are suffering from the drain on your time and your shift in priorities.

- You treat problems in the game with the same urgency as real-life issues, and they infiltrate your daily thoughts and conversations.

Unfortunately, this complex pathology is not yet viewed with the same seriousness as other addictions like drugs and alcoholism. While video game addiction has been profiled in popular shows such as *South Park*, *The Simpsons*, and *King of the Hill*, the media portrayal is usually glossed over by humor instead of delving into the gritty reality. The damage inflicted is never a laughing matter, particularly for those of us on the autism spectrum.

As with changing any problem behavior, the "cure" will not be easy. We are often not able to let go as smoothly as others, and making compromises and accepting change are more challenging. Over time, a new reality will begin to take shape. One of the greatest assets on your road to recovery from any problem behavior will always be the understanding that you have something to offer the non-synthetic social world, and the grass will eventually be greener on the other side. And I am *not* talking about the grass cultivated in *FarmVille*.

THE JOY OF JOB INTERVIEWS

The first chapter of Stephen King's *The Shining* is titled "Job Interview," and the ominous lettering also greets us in the Stanley Kubrick film adaptation. It is an appropriate start to one of the most terrifying works of literature and film ever created. Interviewing for a job can often feel like a horror story, especially if one is on the autism spectrum. The process is a test of overcoming insecurities, sloughing off emotional baggage, and flaunting abilities that may not be evident to the interviewer. It helps considerably when you have the right attitude and a lucid grasp of what is expected of you in this transition to employment. With that said, I would advise you read the first chapter of *The Shining*. It is fictional, but is borrowed from the trenches of reality.

In this scene, the doomed protagonist Jack Torrance is

interviewed for the position of caretaker for the Overlook Hotel and is facing off against a cynical manager. Jack barely survives the interview by politely answering questions that feel like a personal attack. His answers are delivered with smiles that mask a seething dislike for the hotel manager. It is worth pointing out that the interviewer's fears come to fruition because Jack tries to murder his family when the malevolent spirits of the Overlook chip away at his sanity. But on a positive note, Jack did an incredible job during the interview itself and people of all abilities should learn from his example!

Similarly, in the first *Ghostbusters* movie, Winston (Ernie Hudson) is interviewing to be the fourth Ghostbuster. When asked whether he believes in ghosts and other paranormal or supernatural activities, Winston answers the question wisely:

As long as there is a steady paycheck involved, I will believe whatever you tell me to believe.

But in reality, we do not always answer questions with as much poise as these fictional interviewees. In fact, those of us on the autism spectrum are infamous for blowing job opportunities by messing up during the interview process. The consistent failures are usually not an accurate gauge of our abilities and talents. We tend to say the wrong things thanks to our unfiltered honesty, and disclosing our condition is not always a buffer from the same consequences that plague our neurotypical coworkers when they flounder during the interview process, too.

There are some harsh realities that you must absorb before venturing out into the world of employment for the first time or if you are rebuilding your reputation after a disastrous start. It is not about you anymore. It is about the job and what you have to contribute. An employer will hire you because he sees talent or ability. If certain weaknesses are visible, then this may not happen. He must also see you as someone who will enhance the "bottom line" instead of being a threat or problem waiting to happen.

The door swings open with a "whooshing" sound and you are motioned into the office. Ninety-eight percent of the time, an interview starts off with a warm handshake—a gesture dating back to the Middle Ages when a knight extended his hand to indicate he possessed no weapons. But the person interviewing you is neither your friend nor your enemy. And like a bloodhound, he is designed to sniff out flaws and vulnerabilities that may create problems down the road. We may struggle during the interview, but following a few basic tips will keep you from becoming a kamikaze pilot and give you a fair shot at success:

■ **Show up early. Not on time, but early.** While I used to always believe this was just an expression, it represents one of the most efficient ways to destroy an interview from the first second. It does not matter if the interview is at noon and your cell phone clock flashes the identical time. It may not mean a thing if your clock is in conjunction with CNN, the Weather Channel, or the Gatekeepers of International Time Keeping in Greenwich, England. If your interviewer or future boss has his clock set three minutes fast, then you will be three minutes late. Therefore, make it a priority to be early and not just punctual. Leave yourself at least thirty extra minutes to reach the interview considering your trip could be afflicted by construction delays, inclement weather conditions, and just about every other mishap that seems to magically manifest when you need to be somewhere important. If you are going to be late for any reason, the best way to save your hide is to pull over and make a phone call warning them about the probable tardiness. And it is critical to always apologize even if it is not your fault. Then relax and get there when the universe permits it. This is not an ideal scenario, but it is also not ideal to drive eighty-five miles an hour while risking police intervention and endangering the lives of innocent civilians. If you start to panic, then it will not matter if you just barely make it two minutes early. Because barging into the office like Cosmo Kramer will not guarantee a strong start.

■ **Practice proper hygiene and grooming.** Some of us have trouble maintaining a regimen of personal hygiene. On our own time, we may forget to shave and put on a slick coat of deodorant to mask the filthiness like a 1950s beatnik. A job interview will require you to show up in a buttoned-down shirt, clean dress pants, and even a tie. Employers typically believe in the ratio of 1:3 when interviewing new employees. The more slovenly someone looks during the interview, it will be three times worse when the job actually starts.

■ **Do not make money the focus of the interview.** Knowing your salary is important before accepting a position, but making this the second or third question is a foolish idea. If you are dissatisfied with the wages, you can try to negotiate for something better once you've been offered the position. A job in the dietary and kitchen department of a school originally wanted to pay me eight dollars an hour. After politely telling them this was fifty cents *less* than I made eleven years ago at my first summer job in college, they promptly raised it to nine dollars.

■ **Analyze your performance and ask for feedback after repeated failures.** Dissecting your every move may drive you crazy, but not doing so will put you at risk for making the same mistakes over again. You might even want to ask for feedback from your interviewer so that you can try to improve. You may not get a specific or complete response—or you might get a harsh critique that's hard to hear. Bear in mind that eccentricities and rituals are not just limited to those on the autism spectrum. Just about everyone has had a few bad interviews because of the interviewer's peculiarities.

The auto tycoon Henry Ford refused to hire anyone if they put salt on their food before tasting it. It's best to learn what you can from the experience and move on.

■ **Decide whether to disclose.** Disclosing about your Asperger's syndrome is a big decision, one you should consider fully before (not during) the interview. Among the considerations is what the job itself entails. I decided it was not necessary to disclose during my interview for a manufacturing job at a computer plant. People skills are not necessary to assemble parts, and many of the employees seemed nuttier than a holiday fruitcake. But I have always disclosed in environments that involve working with children or similarly sensitive settings. Your disclosure must be augmented by your presentation of the abilities you will bring to the workplace and the desire to improve with consistent feedback (more on this in a moment).

Your employer also does not care about your case of Asperger's, whether you have been bullied in the past, or how hard your life has been. He/she wants to know what you have to offer the company and, most important, will you function as an asset or a liability? Your value is only as great as what you can offer as an employee. It is not about you. It is about the role you will play in the company.

■ **Be confident, but not arrogant.** Overconfidence can be more dangerous than a self-fulfilling prophecy of failure conditioned by a lifetime of setbacks. Never hint that the position is beneath your dignity or that you are more intelligent than your future coworkers. This applies in *all* job interviews even if you are a cum laude graduate from Harvard and are applying to be a men's room attendant. Even if we don't verbalize this overconfidence, it can sometimes be perceived. Be respectful, and make sure you convey that sense of respect.

■ **Use humor only sparingly, and with extreme caution.** While a job interview may take on a casual tone if you and the interviewer develop a rapport with one another, it is critical to remember that you are not out at a bar with an old friend. An interview is still a serious process, and it is best to not use humor. Like a master sushi chef who is cutting the fugu puffer fish to avoid the sections laced with lethal poison, you should only use humor if you are good at it or feel it is necessary to lighten an awkward question. Many of us are also poor with skills involving generalization. If our tactics earn success in one environment, we will believe they are applicable with most other situations and individuals. And if you are lucky enough to earn a laugh, then the best thing to do is immediately quit while you are ahead. As you become more seasoned in the process, you will become better at knowing when to crack a joke and when to keep your mouth shut.

To Tell or Not to Tell

If you represent the extremely slim percentage of those on the autism spectrum with a chameleon-like social talent to adapt to any situation and the stamina to keep it up forever . . . it is probably not necessary to disclose having Asperger's to your interviewer. If something ain't broke, then don't fix it. But if you have a history of never making it past the interview, then you probably have little to lose with the revelation. Always keep in mind, you are disclosing not to excuse yourself from taking responsibility but to strengthen your chances of being successful at the position, if you are hired. Some well-intentioned critics may lobby against disclosure with the reasoning that it is not necessary and will open up a Pandora's box of anxieties for your interrogator. If our uniqueness is going to create contributions and the information will avoid occasional misunderstandings, then I would say go for it. Regardless of whether it is fair, a personnel manager must follow his/her instincts out of professional self-preservation and may reject harmless personality traits if they are not explained.

As we take a deep breath and open up with, "There is something I would like to tell you about myself . . . ," we must remember the Golden Rule about all interviews. KIP! This is not just the name of that slacker, uber-nerdy older brother from the cult movie *Napoleon Dynamite*. It is also the acronym for "keep it positive." Even when revealing a quirk that has been vilified in the past, we may spin a web of reasons why you will still make a good contribution. Here are some examples:

Instead of "I have poor eye contact":

With my Asperger's, I have always had trouble looking at people in the eye, but this has improved over time, especially when I get to know the individual. If I'm not looking at you, then it is nothing personal.

Instead of "certain loud noises make me flap my hands":

I am sometimes startled by loud noises and may overreact by jumping two feet in the air if someone drops a glass or something. But unless you plan to have fire drills almost every day, I am going to be fine 95 percent of the time. If there are any problems, then I'll deal with them and not let them interfere with my job performance.

Instead of "I have trouble using common sense":

When you give me directions, I may ask you to be very specific due to a tendency to misinterpret instructions. For example, if you ask me to get a broom from the store, then I'll ask if you want a long push broom, a broom that sweeps back and forth like the one from The Wizard of Oz, *or one of those battery-powered, Easy Sweep brooms? When I ask questions like this, I am not trying to be a wise guy. I really want to do a good job and get things right.*

Instead of "there is a history of escalating problems and you should warn Human Resources that you might receive sexual harassment complaints":
Any problems from past jobs have been misunderstandings and they almost always were solved when someone brings it to my attention. I welcome criticism from anyone because it helps me do better.

Instead of "I have trouble reading between the lines and getting the joke":
For people with Asperger's syndrome, it is hard to understand sarcasm and read facial expressions. If I do not seem to be getting the message, then all you have to do is nicely tell me.

While it is important to be open about your challenges, there is a mammoth difference between being honest and . . . *being honest.*

With that said, it is a good idea to temporarily drop all unpleasant baggage from past job experiences. A job interview is not a therapy session to rage against all those who have wronged you. The shame, disappointment, or confusion you might feel about how previous interviews or job experiences went off the rails is not what you're here to discuss. You do not have to let it go, but strongly consider putting it on a back burner in this precarious setting.

The Waiting Is the Hardest Part

Following up with a job interview may feel like the subsequent days of an online date. There is silence and a lack of closure. Should you make the first move and follow up, or will your next phone call test someone's patience and end the last shred of hope? You may be tempted to shower them with gifts considering people have responded positively to these gestures in the past. But you should resist this temptation, because a generic card is more appropriate with a few key sentences:

> *It was a pleasure to meet you. I appreciate you taking the time to interview me and telling me about your impressive company. And I look forward to hearing from you with your decision.*

Waiting for a response can be painstakingly frustrating, so it would be in your best interest to continue "seeing other interviewers" while waiting for either an offer or rejection. It has been my personal experience that when an interviewer shakes your hand before saying, "We will get back to you with our answer," it is rarely a promising sign. Some interviewers will have the "Don't call us . . . we'll call you" policy, and you will be forced to wait. You will feel like the pitiful protagonists, Vladimir and Estragon, from the Samuel Beckett play *Waiting for Godot*. A strategy of incremental "backing off" will temper our persistence, which may have been judged as aggressive in the past. Sometimes a complete lack of response is nothing personal, and there are literally hundreds of applicants for a single position. Informing everyone of his or her rejection would be a massive time suck. They could also be lazy, inconsiderate, or pathologically nonconfrontational. Please do yourself a favor by accepting that some jobs will never get back to you with a "yes" or "no" answer. And if "moving on" is not possible, then the lesser of many evils will be to call in monthlong increments until they give you closure. But if these attempts fail, then hopefully you will stop wasting time with someone who does not offer you the courtesy of an answer.

A Few Don'ts

- Bribes and extravagant gifts will rarely help your chances and could quite possibly make them worse. Focus on your skills and potential to contribute, not your willingness to give presents.

- Avoid negativity, anger, and sarcasm. It might not be possible to brush the chip off our shoulder, but perhaps we can compromise by leaving it behind at the door. Or at the very least, keep it behind the wastebasket as it leers harmlessly in eyesight. You are not there to resurrect old vendettas or prove yourself to a callous world. It has stopped being about you unless it has to do with how you may make the office, company, fire department, kitchen, or miscellaneous other workplaces . . . just a little bit stronger with your presence.

- Don't respond to the interviewer's questions before stopping to think first. While your interviewer may show some impatience, your chances will be stronger with hesitation rather than blurting out a stream of verbal sewage. *Sorry for the delay in response. It just takes me a moment to form my thoughts because I want to do my best to show how I may make a valuable contribution.*

- Don't let the past define you. The interviewer may take a condescending look at your résumé (which I hope was drafted with professional assistance).

My stupid parents are tired of me sitting on the couch playing my Nintendo system. I am not taking about the Wii, but the old-school one from the 1980s. They are on my case every damn day! Oh, sorry, sir. I probably should not have said that. It's just that I do not understand what their problem is. You would think it would be enough that I help with the dishes and take care of the cat. I have qualified for social security benefits and this helps. But now they want me to pay more rent, and I need to work at a place like this *[while rolling your eyes] to get more money.*

This might be the real reason, but it won't be your response if you have a snowball's chance in hell of making it past the interview.

I understand your concern that I have not worked in five years. I live with something called Asperger's syndrome, which is the mildest case of autism. Sometimes people with this condition have trouble with making transitions and adjusting. It took me a while to get things together, and I was encouraged to just apply for disability benefits. That was a big mistake, especially because I was capable of working. Even though I have not exactly been getting paid, there has been work experience. For five months I volunteered at the SPCA and showed up on time every day for eight months. I have helped out vendors at walkathons and been responsible. These skills should benefit a real job, and I would show improvement like I did with this volunteer work. Here are a few recommendations from some of these jobs . . .

You can then break out a small library of photocopied papers. If this collection does not yet exist, you will build one. Whenever you move forward after a positive job experience (paid or volunteer), it should become a ritual to present your employer with a small gift of thanks and request a written recommendation. Save the original documents and their contact information in a secure location.

My recommendations are housed in the left plastic pocket of the binder that also holds the business cards collected over the course of eight years.

Keep Learning

Try to view each interview as a learning experience. Sure, in a perfect world it would lead to a job you love, with room to grow into a satisfying career. But even if it's a "one and done" conversation, you can take away lessons that will help you get closer to reaching your ultimate goals.

EMPLOYMENT 101

When consulting with a supported employment program, based in a large hospital, one position that needed to be filled was a pharmacy technician's assistant. We suggested a candidate with ASD to fill the position, with the assurance that there would be a job coach on site at the beginning to make sure things go smoothly. Within the first week, the supervisor at the pharmacy called us exclaiming that she had never had such a great employee in that position; the young man with ASD was quick, efficient, and thorough. Additionally, she mentioned that he had seemingly no interest in the medication he was sorting because he was acutely focused on the expiration dates and was so honest in daily interactions that she had no concerns about him taking anything from the pharmacy. This is a perfect example of how the strengths inherent in individuals with ASDs can lead them to meaningful employment. Dr. Francesca Happe refers to the differences in individuals with ASDs as cognitive biases rather than deficits. If more employers could adopt this perspective, they would be able to embrace the potential of individuals with ASDs as employees and assets to companies.

—Saara Mahjouri, PhD

There is a motivational video on YouTube that has seized my attention, and I have been watching it nonstop. It is called "Be Phenomenal," and the beginning features a little boy applying paste to a fissure on a dusty surfboard tucked away in some woodshed. The next scene shows him cautiously tackling the first of many waves as the powerful narrative voice booms:

You gotta take that big goal, that big dream, that big reality. You gotta take that big reality. And you gotta take small steps to make it manageable. To make it so your dreams become a reality. Think big, dream big, but start small! That's right, start small—remember what I told you. Start where you are with what you have, because what you have is plenty. But the biggest enemy you have to deal with is yourself. There is an old African proverb that says: "If there's no enemy within . . . the enemy outside can do us no harm."

And with those inspirational words . . . start off small and chase streams instead of waterfalls as you pursue your path toward employment. Expecting the possibility of setbacks and making mistakes will go a long way toward moving forward.

The rate of chronic unemployment for those with an autism spectrum disorder is grim. Most statistics vacillate between 80 to 90 percent. These statistics are doubly discouraging because plenty of our most common characteristics can be harnessed to make outstanding contributions in the workplace. Continuing to go on job interviews and being persistent after failures will dramatically tweak your odds. It will also help to have confidence that you have something profound to offer and the resolution to not dwell on past mistakes to the extent that they sabotage your future chances. Eventually, you will achieve that coveted opportunity when an employer gives you a chance because you have impressed them, dressed for the occasion, showed up early, or maybe you are blessed that he/she has had personal experience with Asperger's syndrome. Your interviewer may have a child with Asperger's and see him in your spirit. Or he/she understands that first impressions are often as durable as tissue paper. Achieving the job interview is only half the battle. Now you must find some form of consistency in which to maintain the position and show that you belong in this character-building environment.

For many of us living with Asperger's, employment has proven to be a difficult hurdle to clear. Here are some common issues that may have prevented you from pursuing work in the past:

- Dwelling on negative experiences from past work-related failures

- Choosing career paths that are momentarily or permanently unrealistic

- Having enough of a financial support system and enabling parents

- Suffering in an internal prison of depression or anger

- Being unable to put special interests on a back burner

- Refusing to settle for duties that are "beneath you"

- Fearing to endanger your disability or Social Security benefits

With regard to the last bullet point, there are loopholes that will allow you to maintain employment while still receiving disability benefits to wean yourself away from this common fear. Social Security allows someone to continue receiving financial support as long as you earn less than $1,070 per month. The Social Security Administration's Ticket to Work Program also provides a plethora of incentives to seek employment while receiving disability benefits. All states have some form of a Vocational Rehabilitation (VR) program that can help you navigate the red tape and explore options. In fact, I still receive services from Rehabilitation Support Services (RSS) in New York State, and they have guided me throughout countless personal and professional obstacles.

Many of us are infamous for having a number of mini-careers in our lifetime due to frequent terminations or concluding that the occupation is not right for us. The clay animation protagonist in *Mary and Max* comes to mind because his bizarre résumé included jobs as a garbage collector, condom manufacturer, military inventory analyst, Frisbee maker, subway employee, and communist. As for me, I have had the chance to work in my family's clothing store where I regularly enraged customers with my impulsive comments such as, "Did you just say that your son's name is Damien? Isn't that also the name of the Antichrist from those *Omen* movies?"

I have also been a custodial engineer, a direct care professional at a group home for those with severe disabilities, a fund-raiser for a pediatric AIDS foundation, a substitute teacher, a twelve-hour night shift worker at an IBM manufacturing plant, an assistant funeral home director, an author, a motivational speaker, and a creative writing teacher. Some of these positions floundered due to my undeveloped work ethic and unseasoned social conduct. The one position that was most successful and responsible for lifelong hope happened to be the one that should have exploded in failure back in the summer of 2009.

For some reason, I was an amazing asset to the funeral home. The main clientele were obviously neutral whenever something inappropriate slipped out of my mouth, but most funerals are about the living left behind to mourn for their loved ones. It eventually sunk in that my role was not to serve as a comedian or infuse my Asperger's commentary into a day that was not about me. It was about the embalmed, mortal shell of a human being just beginning his eternal rest. And the families visiting the home who needed tissues and someone to escort them from the car on days when it was raining. This position was most valuable because it taught me how one's weakness can actually double as an authentic strength if we want it badly enough. Perseverance, stamina, and learning from our setbacks are all essential for progress and eventual success.

"Attitude Determines Altitude"

The challenges of employment may seem exhausting, but they can also be liberating. Social acceptance and good performance on the job can be easier to envision and achieve than times where you have been rejected for not being cool enough or failing to dress in the most expensive fashions. Some workplaces resemble a *Saved by the Bell* sitcom with a miscellaneous assortment of extremely dissimilar personalities that somehow coexist. You may be offered the break you deserve for showing up on time, being honest, going above and beyond the line of duty, and exhibiting incremental improvements. Your fellow workers should recognize your efforts to make the day run a little bit smoother and public approval is more attainable. While bullying and rejection can happen anywhere, it is less likely in the workplace when everyone is striving toward shared goals.

If you have minimal to no work experience, then the best thing you should do for yourself is not take on too much at once. Accept a job that may not be ideal in comparison to your lifelong ambitions, but this position could be a vital stepping-stone for these ambitions coming to fruition in the future.

Starting Small

The first of your many career opportunities should be challenging in some ways, but ideally it will involve only a minimal amount of pressure. For example, it might be a better idea to start off as a stock boy at the local supermarket instead of the person at the customer service department who will inevitably be bombarded with a typhoon of complaints and unpredictability. Along the same lines, your first jobs should appeal to at least some of your Asperger's strengths, which probably include a preference for routine.

A lack of pressure does not mean that you have embraced mediocrity or are "a loser" despite your neurotypical classmate who may flaunt his internship for your state congressperson. It merely means you are giving yourself the chance to focus on those qualities of integrity, punctuality, and time management. These are the most endearing qualities for any employee and will serve as the infrastructure for long-term success. You will pad these rudimentary skills with other qualities along the way, but it is wise to devote the start of your career to forging these skills before taking on any other ambitions.

Staying Positive

It will dramatically help your chances if you maintain a positive attitude about any work opportunities. For one thing, I believe it should not be known as "work" because this implies other synonyms that are not so appealing. "Work" is associated with terms like toil, labor, hardship, drudgery, and grind. I prefer the term "employment" because the word "employ" comes with more positive synonyms like utilize, keep busy, and devote. Waking up and reporting to a job five days a week may not be ideal, but neither are the alternative options, even if playing computer games every day sounds like a utopian existence. The body and mind are like any muscle that will atrophy if not put into consistent motion.

Here are a few tips that may help you on the road to fulfilling employment. It would be in your best interest to learn as many lessons as you can through the struggles of your peers who have been educated through the Asperger's School of Draconian Knocks.

■ **Rule 1: Your boss is always right. Rule 2: Your boss is always right.** Kate Palmer is the current executive director of the Global and Regional Asperger Syndrome Partnership (GRASP) and lives with Asperger's syndrome. As is often the case with females, her case is less noticeable than in men and Kate has held down numerous jobs including as a contractor.

Kate always told us, "If a customer asked me to paint his house with pink and green polka dots . . . I would probably ask, 'Are you positive this is what you want?' Then I would get to work if he was set on this paint job."

Unless the task entails clubbing manatees or poses an imminent danger to your health . . . it is necessary to swallow any protest and perform all duties that your boss asks. If you honestly feel your methods make more sense, try voicing these opinions in a ginger and tactful fashion. Let's take the first sentence compared to its polished alternative.

"No, offense. But your way sounds like a big waste of time and will look ridiculous when finished. I want to try my idea instead!"

"Excuse me, Mr. Yardley. I really like your idea, but what are your opinions about this possibility?"

■ **Avoid workplace gossip like the plague.** Gossip or "the act of talking about the business of others" is the black magic of the workplace. There is the temptation to dabble in it, but nothing good can ever come out of discussing personal business. This is where having Asperger's may prove to be an advantage because our inner thoughts may be dancing with science fiction paraphernalia, clay animation movies, nuggets of Thomas the Tank Engine nostalgia, or whatever special interests float your particular boat. The bulk of our cerebral energy, however, should be absorbed with what we need to do in order to make an outstanding contribution as an employee.

Not whether Christina in Human Resources snuck into the broom closet with Justin from Data Processing two months ago for a 9 p.m. liaison. Even if everyone else is relishing the story, it would be in your best interest to avoid the coven of gossip. It will not earn us the social acceptance we deserve and will raise the odds of something inappropriate slipping out that will come back to us in the most egregious fashion.

■ **Maintain realistic social expectations.** *Do not* ask out any of your coworkers or your boss in a romantic fashion. Even if it does not fit the legal definition of sexual harassment (it may or may not), it is always wise to avoid any misunderstandings or feelings of discomfort that do not have to exist. In addition, after you have developed a strong rapport with your neurotypical coworkers, it would be wise to ask them for guidance about the rules hidden beneath actual rules in the employee handbook, to gain more insight and perspective on what is and is not appropriate. Though in the end, you alone are responsible for making good decisions. Don't expect to be best friends with your coworkers. Johnny Carson and Ed McMahon shared the stage of *The Tonight Show* for thirty years, but they rarely if ever socialized outside of the studio. The same is true for the late movie critics Gene Siskel and Roger Ebert. They maintained a cordial relationship while working, but nothing more. Similarly, do not take it personally if your coworkers reject offers to go out to lunch or walk the local bike trail even if your intentions are obviously platonic. And never push the issue. Most people value their free time and prefer to spend it with family or focusing on tasks that they could never address on the job. They also might not want to spend their "downtime" with people or activities that remind them of work.

■ **Understand the difference between gentle teasing and bullying.** Your coworkers may detect your naïveté and have a little bit of fun once in a while at your expense. At one job where I was working an overnight shift, some young women concealed themselves under a table and whispered my name as I frantically paced around the kitchen thinking the voices were caused by my state of sleep-deprived delirium. At another place, a coworker exploited my diligence of answering phones and called the number in the adjacent room. When I picked up the phone, she promptly called the number in the other room. For about ten minutes, I was rushing back and forth like a caffeinated hamster on his wheel. These pranks were innocuous and very sporadic. But our history of being tormented in the past may make us sensitive to such stunts. Therefore, if some teasing pushes all of your hot buttons, then it may be a good idea to politely address the issue and explain that these nonmalicious shenanigans interfere with your work performance.

■ **Prepare yourself for limited second chances.** The workplace does not offer infinite "do overs" and is not forgiving of continuous mistakes. Compared to school or home life, it is a different ballgame with limited chances to step up to the same plate.

I never played in Little League growing up, but I imagine that I would have been one of those misfit, *Bad News Bears*–type of players who struck out repeatedly. Perhaps I would have cried or thrown my bat in an outburst of displaced anger. But there would have been other chances and eventually a home run might have transpired, followed by an explosion of cheers. Despite having a reputation as a troublemaker throughout school, there was always the next day to pursue redemption and wipe the slate clean. Part of being an adult is accepting there will be lasting consequences for truly inappropriate conduct that creates a sense of liability for the employer and interferes with the comfort zone of coworkers. You should always assume there will not be another chance if you exhibit poor judgment. As Sylvester Stallone says in the underappreciated 1980s gem *Over the Top*, "The world meets nobody halfway!"

Actions that are subject to termination include but are not limited to the following:

- Temper tantrums
- Making impulsive threats (even if you are obviously not serious)
- Reciting jokes that have the potential to offend people of different races, religions, creeds, or other aspects of identity or lifestyle

- Becoming belligerent about performing duties essential to the job or about anything else

- Persistent complaining

- Chronic lateness

- Repeated cell phone and social media usage on the job

On a related note, individuals with Asperger's often have a talent for thinking outside the box. This can be a huge asset for employers, but it can also be dangerous. Be sure to run your wild ideas and unconventional solutions by your supervisor before implementing them. With proper approvals and supervision, you are likely to be rewarded for your originality. Without these forms of guidance, you might find yourself in hot water for not playing by the rules.

■ **Beware of the evils of complacency.** One of the worst things that can happen in your job experiences is growing too comfortable with your situation and forgetting that you are at the workplace. You are becoming friendly with your boss and have dropped the formalities of addressing him as "sir" or "mister." The Berlin Wall of professionalism has toppled and you have relaxed the filter mechanism among your coworkers. Then the wrong wisecrack tumbles from your lips like a gaggle of malevolent clowns from a circus car. Think before you speak, and always keep in mind the expectations and standards of your surroundings.

Always remember that you are at a job and your friendly coworkers are not the same "friends" who usually show mercy when something inappropriate slips out.

■ **Know when it's time to move on.** Success will come from knowing you have value and purpose when others give you a chance. As I've said, it's good to start small. But once you've put in the hard work and paid your dues, it's also important to set our sights on the next challenge, so that we continue to learn and grow.

We crave the fruits of life that appear to come with more ease for neurotypicals. And when we finally achieve that elusive romantic partner and job, our gratitude is so potent that it may keep us from reaching for higher ideals. Therefore, there is the danger of remaining in situations that are a Catch-22 with little hope of significant improvement. Here are some signs that it is time to move on and raise your standards:

- Being strung along with empty promises for raises and promotions

- Suffering physiological and psychological effects exacerbated by your work, such as headaches, stomachaches, depression, and anger

- Being taken advantage of or underappreciated by coworkers who want you to cover their shifts without any gratitude or the return of a rare favor

- Performing the same tasks beneath your intellectual abilities without any expansion. We must start off at the bottom but eventually be allowed to move forward once we have proven ourselves

■ **Avoid real-world distractions. Like your *phone*.** Most of us are chained to some kind of electronic device these days, in many cases a phone that functions like a miniature computer, camera, and video arcade. The pleasures and possibilities are endless. Plenty of employers are aware of this temptation and have a zero tolerance policy for personal electronics that do not pertain to the job requirements. This is easier said than done and may be the equivalent of going cold turkey from a narcotic. There were times when I would sneak the phone in with me to the bathroom to get my "fix" while simultaneously taking care of bodily functions. If your job makes it clear that a phone is off-limits during work hours, please resist the temptation by locking it in your car while giving your family the work number for emergencies. Before you do anything that is recreational or does not contribute to the task at hand, take a deep breath and think.

■ **Find appropriate ways to spend your downtime.** A common problem for those on the autism spectrum is inappropriate uses of downtime at our place of work. Even during a legitimate break where you are allowed to check your phone and have Internet privileges, one must be extremely careful. If you are not sure, always ask whether it is appropriate to go on certain web pages like Match.com . . . YouTube . . . and Facebook. If these web pages are off-limits, then *do not* try to get away with it because all of these pages are archived in the browser. You will be caught and possibly terminated when there is an investigation into who logged onto these forbidden sites. Everything you search for is archived in the company's browser. And you never know who is looking over your shoulder at your mobile device.

If you *are* allowed on YouTube and Facebook during breaks, use good judgment when choosing your manner of entertainment. Typing in the keywords "best sex scenes in Demi Moore movies" is not the greatest idea and could also be a liability for the job site because someone is using their equipment to look up "pornography." If you are going to watch any videos, I beg of you to make them as innocuous as possible.

■ **Think before you post!** There was once a man with a slight build and an oversized proboscis. He was also cursed with the Surname from Hell and was probably the recipient of a childhood filled with incessant teasing. Yet he still managed to overcompensate for these obstacles by serving New York state for many years and becoming a confidant of President Bill Clinton. He was once a viable candidate for New York City mayor and married one of the most beautiful, ambitious women in the world. Somehow, he managed to screw everything up (twice!) with a Twitter scandal that should teach all of us that what we put on the Internet may have a lasting consequence.

We must follow Anthony Weiner's tragedy by analyzing our Facebook posts that are inspired by emotion, especially if they pertain to a bad day at work. Or include inflammatory subjects and jokes with racial or otherwise offensive overtones. It does not matter whether something is up there for a second before you come to your senses. Even if your coworkers are not on your Facebook page, there is always somebody who knows somebody when you decide to post:

Rough day at work today, guys! My boss can be an enormous prick!

The advantage to seeking employment is oftentimes a sudden acceleration of maturity and an opportunity to manage some of the less desirable Asperger's characteristics. You will eventually be able to let go of some of the nonpriorities that slice away energy from your work responsibilities. This includes special interests that are no longer useful when time becomes more scarce (and therefore more valuable). Regular employment will take away an excess of idle time when there was once ample room to dwell on unhealthy thoughts. You will procure a greater understanding of other people's points of view and why they may have treated you a certain way. I used to rage against individuals who did not put in the energy to maintain a friendship with me as I was home twiddling my thumbs while sending them emails on Facebook. Now, the tables have turned, and I am finally receiving a potent dose of my own medicine as unemployed friends contact me all day long. The source of my annoyance is not from hypocritical contempt for their well-intentioned actions. It is due to the discomfort of having to look at myself in the mirror and understand how past conduct may have made others feel.

Some people believe that immaturity is a character defect. But I believe this view is incorrect, because immaturity is simply a sign that one has not had the chance to take on enough experiences to learn a new way of behaving. The merits of maturity must be earned by taking on new experiences and being open to their life lessons. In addition to offering these learning experiences, employment will help you feel a surge of pride for feeling productive and focused on a meaningful goal. More than anything, employment is a means to prove your potential to the world while building the fiscal resources to taste the sweeter fruits of life.

THE D-WORD
(DISCLOSURE)

Disclosure. The term is synonymous with the erotic thriller written by Michael Crichton and adapted into a film starring Demi Moore and Michael Douglas. Like its 1988 predecessor, *Fatal Attraction*, which also features Michael Douglas being pursued by a beautiful woman, it shows that the unseen grass is not always greener and that the loneliest of us should indeed be careful what we wish for. But in the Asperger's community, the term takes on a more somber notion when it comes to opening up about having Asperger's syndrome outside of the haven we have built for ourselves. Disclosure is the fragile artistry of revealing that you have this sometimes difficult, often beautiful condition and how to best educate the public. When do you disclose and whom do you want to tell? And when is it best to just remain silent?

My father has always told me, "Never live with regret, Jesse." He always said this whenever I faced the cliché of two diverging paths in the woods. One path would be harder and the other would offer a quick-fix solution but came with the Faustian consequences that were often long term. Even after learning about my diagnosis at age fourteen, my parents thought it would be prudent to keep it a secret as though they were still walking on the fringes of denial. Disclosure would have made our lives easier because family members would have at least had a chance to understand. Even now, when I think back to that time, regrets are forever swirling around my head like flakes of asbestos.

Some Misunderstandings Are Avoidable

Looking back on my adolescence, there were quite a few times when a family member responded harshly to my behavior, not knowing the reason behind it. The worst episode was probably the night at a New York City restaurant when my cousin was talking about getting braces in the near future. I blurted out, "Oh, God! Braces were the absolute bane of my existence. They were like a gigantic chain dragging from my teeth." As usual, I did not know when to stop and continued to rant about the evil headgear that looked like the front guard of a football helmet had been molded by pipe cleaners. Another relative's face contorted in disgust as she cried out, "Oh, God! You should be very grateful you had braces! I had to get them as an adult and [another cousin] is going to also have them next year. How do you think he feels about what you are saying?!" The harangue went on for a few minutes. There were similarly disapproving confrontations from other relatives, many of which have left permanent scars.

It is easy to throw these relatives under the bus and clump them together as villains without acknowledging how different things would have been if they had known. Just like we would have gone easier on family members if we had known *their* closely held struggles and challenges.

The Power of a Support Group

Disclosure is easier within an autism support group where there is less fear and judgment. Unlike in the population at large, no one within an Asperger's support group will question whether the condition exists (or is an invention of pop psychology). Opening up to peers with the same diagnosis can serve as the baby steps toward more frequent, public disclosure, especially when you are just learning about having Asperger's. My Coven of Aspies—which is part of GRASP, the Global and Regional Asperger Syndrome Partnership—meets in a Manhattan doctor's office where a motley group of warriors assembles with a collective sigh of relief. We cease walking on eggshells as we do in the real world, and the gathering becomes a safe refuge. The personalities in my group are eclectic, including an exotic-looking woman with straggly hair whose unique looks have landed her regular work as a movie extra. Nobody is fazed when she removes her shoes and socks to perform various contortions on the yoga mat she totes around. She is not constricted by worrying what we will think. It is a beautiful form of acceptance. Another man is morbidly obese and lacking in many social graces. In general, members are not always the most polite, politically correct, or self-aware, but we do not judge each other for these shortcomings. A few determined members eventually show signs of progress, which motivates the rest of us to keep up. It takes a lot to be banned from the group, but there are exceptions. Those who are not welcome back are usually individuals who squander second chances on their fifth chances. Any outrageous outbursts are neither molded nor polished by constructive criticism, and the banning is almost always self-inflicted. It is another jabbing reminder that having autism will not make us immune to consequences, but the mercy that is not omnipresent in the neurotypical society is usually found in our group meetings.

The facilitators of the GRASP groups also have Asperger's, and they serve as role models in addition to group leaders. A new discussion topic is assigned every month that ranges from dating, family relationships, employment, and anger issues, to disclosure. The gatherings about disclosure are usually the most attended meetings since it is such a pressing and important topic.

Why Disclose?

Disclosure may always be on our minds, but it is difficult to take the plunge because we are also exposing our vulnerability. Will our revelation negatively alter what was once a stable relationship? Will it be the first and final straw that dooms a job interview that otherwise would have been saved? Is this new information going to create more misunderstandings and fear that did not have to exist? The ball is placed in someone else's court, which is a frightening concept.

Perhaps you should think of disclosure as a fine net to filter out those who are ill-equipped to handle your uniqueness. Or at least give it a chance. Do you really want someone to be part of your life who is going to cave in to knee-jerk fear, judgment, and stereotypes? If it was not the revelation about Asperger's syndrome, then it could have very well been something else just as petty that would most likely have driven this person away.

> *I'm selfish, impatient and a little insecure. I make*
> *mistakes, I am out of control and at times hard to handle.*
> *But if you can't handle me at my worst, then you*
> *sure as hell don't deserve me at my best.*
> —Marilyn Monroe

In some situations, disclosure seems like the lesser of two evils. It can come out of necessity. You might want to think about disclosing if the following things are happening:

- Constant and unexplained rejections from job opportunities

- Fair and unfair criticism for traits related to Asperger's

- Judgments from family members disgusted with your failures, alleged lack of ambition, unexplained behavior, or other perceived flaws

- Sporadic harassment from authority figures over misunderstandings

- Failures in analyzing social cues from the neurotypical community

- Benign quirks that are seen as threats

Disclose to Whom?

With our troubles involving generalization, we should understand that disclosure should be reserved for those who are an established part of our lives or have the potential to become consistent fixtures. It is probably not necessary to disclose to pizza deliverymen, mechanics, the postal carrier, and others who come and go without a recurring, important role in our existence. The individuals worth considering disclosing to include, but are certainly not limited to:

- Clergy members

- Bosses and coworkers

- First dates (especially if there are no fireworks and you have nothing to lose)

- Immediate family members and other somewhat close relations

- Best friends

- College professors and other instructors

- Job coaches

You should feel more comfortable, with less risk of long-term consequences, when respectfully disclosing at an establishment where you are a paying customer. A restaurant or clothing store is designed to meet the needs of their customer regardless of whether he/she is in a wheelchair or endowed with harmless eccentricities. Do you prefer to be served by the same waitress every visit to your favorite diner? Or perhaps you are in noticeable agony from the fluorescent lights in a convenience store that quiver with the ambiance of an abandoned prison still inhabited by one covert murderer on the loose. These preferences and sensitivities do not give you the right to pitch a tantrum when your favorite waitress takes a vacation. Or blurting out, "Must you turn the lights on so high every f***ing day?!" But you should always have the right to gingerly and respectfully voice your request or ask for a reasonable modification. One of the reasons that I continue visiting my favorite local coffee shop is because the virtuous baristas work around my phobia of waste (which I developed after seeing a documentary about a Texas-sized circle of garbage rotting in the Pacific Ocean). They automatically place my items on a plate or hand it to me in a film of tissue paper when I remind them that a paper bag is not necessary to make the four-foot trip to a vacant table. As long as you are not inconveniencing the staff or other customers, your request (and disclosure by way of explanation) is usually worth the effort. For the handful of managers who choose to be abrasive, it is prudent to remind them that there are plenty of people that could easily treat me as a "stalker" or "annoyance" for free and are thus undeserving of my hard-earned money. Perhaps you should send the same message by simply leaving without explanation. "Communicate with your feet."

How to Disclose?

Like asking out someone to your first high school dance, your first disclosure will be the most nerve-racking. What will help is a strong opening line that sets the stage for a positive dialogue. Maybe some of these ideas are enough to get you started. Ideally, you will come up with some original ones of your own:

Have you ever watched The Big Bang Theory? *Remember we talked about what a jerk Sheldon Cooper is? Well . . . don't worry because I am not like that. But there are qualities about him that are similar to a disorder I have called Asperger's syndrome.*

I am getting the feeling that some employees are a little nervous around me. Even if I am just being paranoid, you should know something about myself anyway.

Remember when I made Brittany really uncomfortable last month because I gave her red roses on her birthday? You explained that red roses apply to romance, which I had not considered. But there is another reason that I made this mistake.

I am sure you have heard of Albert Einstein and Thomas Edison. Even though Einstein was the smartest man who ever lived, he was extremely absentminded and would sometimes forget to put on socks and walked into the middle of football games while thinking about equations. I am not *saying that I am a genius, but Einstein supposedly had a mild form of autism like me. And . . .*

The opening line should be nonconfrontational and perhaps a little humorous, and the entire dialogue should close with a promise to always be open to future feedback. By removing the main source of mystery and misunderstandings, you will be paving the way to move forward productively.

Disclosure may come out of necessity when we realize that our actions have an impact on those around us and have the capacity to create a blanket of fear within the neurotypical public within our own communities. You may know that your inability to conform is neither a threat nor a cause for concern, because most of us do not wake up in the morning to scheme about how we can make people a little more uncomfortable than the previous day. *How can I enhance my creepiness just an inch more than yesterday?* If you get the sense that people are uncomfortable around you, it may be just your imagination fueled by paranoia or the lifelong aftershocks of past baggage. With that said, the greatest tool that will help you carve out a productive existence is inviting community members to provide feedback when necessary.

And in a world of social homeostasis . . . there would be compassion for everyone who means well and poses no real threat to society. People would understand that fearing anyone who seems abnormal makes as much sense as believing that people who are superficially "normal" must always be harmless and good. But as you grow older, reality should slowly permeate your consciousness, and you will understand that some members of society are conditioned to fear anything that deviates from the norm. Here are some innocuous behaviors that may be perceived as "threats" by uneducated members of the community:

- Hand flapping and other forms of stimming activities

- Initiating conversations with children and visiting age-inappropriate venues of recreation such as children's water parks

- Mistaking casual acquaintances for best friends by becoming overly familiar

- Giving unsolicited gifts to these acquaintances on holidays or birthdays

- Meltdowns brought on by sensory issues like loud music

- A monotone voice and unusual facial expressions

- Frustration escalating into more aggressive forms of communication such as foot stomping and yelling

- Failures with generalization that permit the telling of raunchy jokes where they are no longer appropriate

- Getting caught staring at someone who is highly attractive

- Talking too loudly and fast

- Absentmindedly wearing inflammatory clothing, such as a T-shirt with Arabic lettering

The worst of our meltdowns will recede if we pursue life experiences that allow us to garner maturity. Despite any phenomenal improvements, we would do ourselves a disservice to "let go" and assume we are "cured." Relapses may occur not just due to Asperger's, but because we are as human as everyone else, and we may become complacent with our progress.

Not a "Get out of Consequences Free" Card

It is important to be accountable for our behavior under all circumstances and never fall into that trap of brushing it off on Asperger's. But the reality remains that because we are as human as everyone else and struggle with Asperger's syndrome, we could very well engage in some impulsive or unconscious conduct that makes other people uncomfortable. These feelings of discomfort are rarely brought to the surface right away because the standards of communication are rapidly altered in adulthood. Fellow adults often communicate by *not* communicating and become extremely nonconfrontational. We may be rejected by potential romantic partners through neutral answers such as, "I am really busy this month. Maybe some other time." When our behaviors provoke discomfort in public, these feelings are not brought to our attention right away. The public may communicate their discomfort through dirty looks, not answering the phone if they recognize our number, lack of eye contact, and a flat affect when answering questions. It is difficult to figure out whether this is an attitude from someone having a bad day or something we inadvertently did to create this discomfort. Sometimes we find our answer the hard way.

There was one young man with a challenging case of Asperger's syndrome who was nearly expelled from his high school for repeatedly saying "hello" to a girl he wanted to befriend. He always acknowledged her while passing in the congested hallway or popping his head inside a classroom. The girl always rolled her eyes or pretended not to hear him. The boy had enough sympathetic students looking out for him. Maybe a few tried to instill the social wisdom of not squandering your kindness on those who do not acknowledge your existence.

"What is the big deal? Why can't you just say 'hello' back to him?"

She barked, "No way! He is weird and I just want him to leave me alone!"

Eventually, the girl decided she had enough and her parents went to the superintendent in an effort to have the young man moved to another school. A parade of hearings followed to determine whether a threat actually existed to warrant expulsion. The matter was eventually resolved without additional punishment, but it was a *very* close call. In this case, a young adult was granted clemency and allowed to finish his high school career. I have not yet heard the girl's side of the story, which may contain the omitted details of unrelenting phone calls and other serious forms of harassment. But it is still wise to assume that a little more education and careful disclosure could have taken the edge off the girl's fears. And, of course, the hapless young man's suffering.

There are also horror stories about those with Asperger's who have been unceremoniously terminated from jobs after unresolved misunderstandings are allowed to mushroom even further. Perhaps you have even experienced them yourself. These failures are costly not just for the self-confidence of the individual but may result in disability payments for someone who is not disabled, or difficulty justifying future attempts at productive employment. Erasing the stigma of liability may not happen overnight, but the autism community will be able to shave off slivers of anguish when these misunderstandings do occur.

I've had my share of misunderstandings that led to unfortunate experiences—times when my atypical behavior led others to think I was up to no good, causing them to take action, threatening to fire me, banning me from the premises, and other ways of making it clear I was no longer welcome. In each of these incidents, I was not given the benefit of the doubt, nor was I informed early on that my quirks and odd habits were becoming a problem.

Such experiences should teach us that we should always strive to make people feel comfortable, and that respect and communication must be a two-way effort, for everyone's sake. We should disclose not to excuse bouts of bad behavior, but to provide an open door for addressing fears that often can easily be resolved. At the beginning, you may be tempted to disclose only to diffuse uncomfortable situations that may have been self-inflicted. Unfortunately, it never worked for me because the response was often along the lines of, "Is inappropriate behavior part of your autism, too? Do people with autism have a staring problem, too?" A cocked head and condescending sneer almost always followed these comments.

If I could repeat these many encounters over again, I would have said a few more things that could have earned more understanding:

- Occasionally, inappropriate behavior is exacerbated by my condition. Furthermore, I am as human as you and everyone else. But I am very sorry for what happened and will work harder.

- Most of the time, I do not know that I am making people uncomfortable, and I am not a mind reader. If you bring issues to my attention, then I will immediately stop.

- I want to do better and will do whatever I can to work with you.

It is now extremely rare for me to run into these situations, but this is partially due to proactive actions of inoculation. I sometimes carry around a card or letter stating that I have Asperger's in case I need to explain my uniqueness or calm any concerns. The letter lists my history of troubles, a little bit about Asperger's, and gives out my cell phone/email information so that store personnel may easily get in touch with me if desired.

Feedback Is Essential

Professional drivers sometimes have a bumper sticker with the caption, "How's my driving?" along with a phone number so that the public has the option of making complaints about minor annoyances like tailgating and more serious violations, such as hit-and-run accidents. This is a courtesy to the public, and studies have shown this results in 22 percent fewer accidents and lower insurance premiums. Similarly, I think it would make sense to create a card for those in the Asperger's community who are experiencing a challenging transition into adulthood. Or merely at the phase in life in which behaviors have stopped being "cute." They may be doing their absolute best at this current level of maturity but still have a mountain of progress left to ascend. The card could be emblazoned with capped calligraphy that asks, "HOW'S MY BEHAVIOR?" complete with a number to reach a trusted counselor or parent (to share anonymous feedback—either positive or negative). The back would contain a rudimentary definition of Asperger's syndrome or autism spectrum disorders as well as some of the traits that may exist. It would serve four critical functions:

- Addressing problems before they rage out of control

- Showing the public that we have concern for their comfort level

- Reminding ourselves that we should show ourselves some of the mercy that will hopefully come from a few sympathetic members of our community

- Infusing accountability to compensate for a lack of maturity to help us make good choices. I am not sure about the rest of you, but if someone had an invitation to contact one of my family members, then I would certainly hesitate before acting

Self-Advocacy

Another dream of mine is to create something called the Autism Self-Advocacy Network (ASAN) to advocate for our peers who are still in the throes of Asperger's and suffering from the draconian consequences. These repercussions (especially the first one) should have the effect of molding us to do a little bit better. When consequences take the form of enduring punishments that make it difficult to bounce back, it becomes almost impossible to find a purposeful place in society. The ASAN could be a database of individuals who have already "walked the walk" and will be a source of guidance for those willing to reach out to us for life coaching.

We should also create something called the Army of Self-Advocate Power (ASAP) to find meaning from our past suffering that may consume us with regret if not put to a constructive purpose. As this acronym suggests, any damage could be reversed in a swifter manner with our intervention. My vision for the future involves a highly organized network of our peers who have succeeded in building a life and put the worst of their anguish behind them through reaching incremental levels of maturity.

When problems plagued us in the past, there may not have been someone by our side to advocate for our long-term potential. We most likely did not have character witnesses who could help society distinguish a benign mistake from a malignant threat. We may have had advocates such as job coaches, but nobody who could help the public understand what it means to be on the autism spectrum.

The ASAP will be a directory of former "lost souls" who rebuilt their lives through positive changes in behavior and attitude. Some of us will hopefully be included within this network someday. As we celebrate this escape from pain and failure brought on by ancient behaviors, we can also help our peers who are still battling demons with little to show for their efforts. The days of childhood stickers and other accolades for tiny accomplishments fade away when adulthood takes over. A little compassion and a few "breaks" can go a long way to helping set a course for long-term success. Private funding would also allow us the opportunity to travel and intervene in court cases where the defendant shares our struggles, as our presence becomes the perfect buffer to a lack of education.

Until this powerful resource comes into existence, we must learn to advocate for ourselves. If you are having trouble letting go of old habits and anguish from the past, then you will have a greater incentive to learn the skills of disclosure so that you may help others understand your struggle and good intentions. When you have become seasoned in the art of self-advocacy, I hope you will pay it forward by helping peers who are still floundering. Over time, we will cease thinking of it as revealing our "disability." We will be disclosing on the fact that we are sometimes misunderstood but are otherwise incredible and able-bodied members of society.

MAKING YOUR MARK

We are convinced, then, that autistic people have their place in the organism of the social community. They fulfill their role well, perhaps better than anyone else could, and we are talking of people who as children had the greatest difficulties and caused untold worries to their care-givers.

—Hans Asperger

There were many advantages in attending a college as amazing as Hobart and William Smith. These were benefits experienced by students of all abilities. Our college president, Mark Gearan, was the director of the Peace Corps under the Clinton Administration, and his family took me under their wing, which was the perfect buffer to any challenges. There were often celebrities visiting the college such as the Clintons, famous writers, and other household names that broke free from the television to shake my hand.

The May 2004 commencement ceremonies at Hobart and William Smith Colleges started with the words of our speaker, Chris Matthews. He was addressing hundreds of students who would succeed based on the tools acquired and sharpened during four years of college. But there would also be some harsh realities that we would have to contend with, including those that were unpredictable such as the Great Recession.

Mr. Matthews encouraged us to "get into the game." He used an analogy about a young boy who is shorter than most of his classmates but nurses ambitions to excel on the basketball court. He waits in vain on the sidelines during practices every afternoon wearing the jersey gifted mainly out of sympathy by the assistant coach who hopes this annoying kid will eventually give up. When the team finally leaves, this forlorn boy practices by himself with layups and dribbling. One day, a player sprains his ankle and is forced to sit out for a while. The coach looks around in frustration because two other players are also absent due to other commitments. He glances at the boy and grudgingly invites him to substitute for the player. The team collectively rolls their eyes but tolerates his unwelcomed presence.

This boy is not great . . . but he is not bad. He takes directions and is willing to do whatever it takes to show that he belongs and can be taken seriously as a competitor. Over time, his teammates start to think of him less as an imposition and more of an asset to the team. It is going to take a long time, but he will continue picking away at it with the understanding that every feat will have the outcome of sustaining momentum. Our abilities may not have to do with athletics, but the analogy applies to any other area. "Getting into the Game" is built on the confidence that we can make a contribution when others give us a fighting chance. It may also entail embracing situations that provoke discomfort for the sake of becoming just a little bit more skilled than before.

In order for us to persist, it is necessary to move past some of the unfair stereotypes and attributes that have contributed to a damaged self-esteem. While bullying and rejection may not be as frequent a challenge as it was when we were younger, we remember the standards that were both daunting and impossible. We were judged harshly for how we dressed, our flat affect, our naïveté, and anything else perceived as a weakness, while our more redeeming characteristics were often ignored. Adulthood is time for these overlooked qualities to rise to the surface and shine. The following checklist may be considered common Asperger's traits that would make a contribution in your community:

☐ Integrity

☐ Honesty (The good kind. As Dr. Temple Grandin says, "You cannot tell other people they are stupid, even if they really are stupid.")

☐ Punctuality

☐ Conscientiousness

☐ Perseverance

☐ Focus

There are certain careers we need to give up on because of the unusual social skills that are needed for success. A CIA profiler is probably not in the cards because we would fail as human lie detectors interviewing double agents. But to believe that a lack of social skills will prevent us from succeeding anywhere is a huge disservice and insult to our population. Our persistence will enhance those skills like a muscle.

Your Dreams Must Include a Dash of Reality

It is also a common fallacy that making a significant contribution can only pertain to anything that results in fame and fortune. Nearly every individual, whether neurotypical or autistic, goes through a phase where they dream of being a famous screenwriter, movie star, architect, singer, or any other profession that is over-glorified in our pop culture society. My youthful aspirations were to be a famous movie actor, but I had enough cognizance of reality to know it would never be as a dashing leading man like Harrison Ford or Pierce Brosnan. I accepted that a more realistic ambition would be a hardworking character actor who adds drama but doesn't end up on the movie poster. Of course, the reality is that most of us are not destined to be movie stars, but those of us with Asperger's tend to hold on to this stardust longer than our neurotypical peers. Finding my voice as a writer, speaker, and advocate has satisfied my craving for the spotlight. For those of you who are having trouble letting go of your lofty visions, there are other ways to get a little closer to your dream, while staying grounded in reality. Achieving your ambitions, whatever they are, is not going to happen overnight, and it is foolish to only focus on these goals without having a more practical Plan B in place.

■ **See yourself as a role model from day one.** Sometimes it can be as simple as setting a good example and showing that your behavior has progressed with leaps and bounds over the years. Be consistent and always try to be a person of your word. Society is aware of us as having a disability, and the characteristics deemed to be negative have more lasting power. Let's collectively step up to the plate to show that our positive characteristics may eventually overshadow any rocky moments. Those individuals who are floundering in the throes of immaturity or more challenging cases can look toward the future because they will benefit from the support provided by us. Eventually, they will also take their rightful place as new role models.

■ **Start small.** It is important to aim high, but it's also necessary to pay the bills and pay "our dues" in the world of work. Maintaining some sort of steady income, even if the work itself does not bring us joy or do justice to our talents, is an important stepping-stone for later success. For example, I started out serving twelve-hour shifts at a computer plant. Accepting situations that are less than ideal is not a conspiracy against those with Asperger's syndrome. Just about every successful actor is able to share horror stories about what they had to do to etch out a living in between going on auditions. Warren Beatty, for instance, tried to get his foot in the door by accepting a position catching mice in the National Theatre in Washington, DC. Like me, Whoopi Goldberg also worked at a funeral home. (She also worked as a phone sex operator, but I would not suggest that career for anyone on the spectrum, because we are generally not great at avoiding scams and maintaining our privacy.)

If you want to become the next Nobel Prize–winning chemist, then pursue this goal, but do not be afraid to start off your journey cleaning mucus out of test tubes as a laboratory assistant. That's the way the world works.

■ **Discover where your talents will be appreciated.** When we focus only on the rejections and knee-jerk first impressions, we tend to miss out on the areas where our abilities will be embraced because they are more rare within the neurotypical population. Numerous individuals with Asperger's thrive in the computer science field because of our ability to scrutinize massive amounts of data and pinpoint the small errors that need to be corrected. The German software company SAP is even hiring individuals on the autism spectrum. According to MSN News on May 22, 2013, SAP has already employed six individuals as software testers in Bangalore, India, as part of their pilot program, and BBC reported that the company expects 1 percent of its sixty-five thousand global workforce to be people with autism by 2020.

■ **Start a support group.** Many of us do not respond to traditional psychotherapy, and it can also be cost-prohibitive. For many of us, it might be a healthier alternative to find clusters of likeminded people who can compare notes and offer supportive advice. There are numerous support groups all over the country for parents and individuals with Asperger's. If there is not yet one in your community, it might be time for you to step up to the plate and create one inside a church, library, or anyplace else generous enough to lend you their space. Be the hero who puts a tourniquet on some of the isolation and self-sabotage that is found in adulthood. You may not be able to solve everyone's problems, but you can be a sounding board and offer support to help individuals get back on their feet. Support groups should do the following:

- Create structure and support for those with a limited social circle

- Provide recreational activities and organized weekend outings

- Brainstorm in order to solve common problems related to organization, dating, job development, etc

- Build a safe space for people to confide about their struggles without judgment

Building a support group will not be an easy task, but there are numerous resources available. Even if only four individuals show up for the first gathering . . . those are four whole people who finally have more motivation to get through the week and a reason to wake up earlier on a Saturday morning during times of unemployment.

■ **Learn to make compromises.** Nobody gets what they want right away, and flexibility is critical to success and fulfillment in the adult world. There was one woman at my support group who only wanted to be an obstetrician's assistant that rubs the lubricant jelly on the stomachs of women. The rest of us pointed out the hurdles that could prevent this dream from coming to fruition. We are sadly not famous for our bedside manner, and how could she develop or even fake the skills to know the right thing to say? Could she have the self-control and stamina to react gingerly when working with women on the emotional roller coaster of carrying a baby to full term? It takes a Pollyanna with Hannibal Lector–like intuition to become what someone needs. In the end, she accepted our suggestions to shadow an actual assistant while performing basic tasks under his/her supervision before taking on more challenging expectations.

■ **Remember that "When you help others . . . you are really helping yourself."** We tend to be focused on our own problems, struggles, and achievements. Are we fitting in enough, working hard enough, getting closer to our goals? Sometimes, progress and growth can come from sharing your time and talents with those in our community. Volunteering can prove to be a natural high, especially when working with disadvantaged individuals, the elderly, animals, or others on the autism spectrum. Dr. Temple Grandin speaks about the summers as a teenage girl when her boarding school instructors allowed her to take responsibility for a horse, which produced a new sense of self-worth. My salvation also came in the most unlikely of places. During times of subzero self-esteem, I began to donate blood regularly at a local hospital. The amiable staff made me feel comfortable, and knowing that my vital fluids had something to do with giving a stranger another chance was enough to buffer some dark times.

These days, I have become something of a known figure in the autism community in my area. I visit frequently with young children who are struggling to find their way. (Yes, we have been known to dance to the *SpongeBob SquarePants* Jellyfish Jam.) Helping kids and their parents feel better in the moment and more hopeful about the future serves to give me purpose as well as a sense of pride and accomplishment.

Become a New Stereotype

Hans Asperger did research on a small group of students when he wrote his dissertation back in 1944. He noticed that while his students had difficulties with empathy and understanding social cues, there was extraordinary compensation in talents related to mathematics and science. Dr. Asperger's theories were finally embraced by American society in 1994 when Asperger's syndrome was finally added to the *Diagnostic and Statistical Manual of Mental Disorders* (DSM-IV). Sadly, Hans Asperger died in 1980, just before his studies were widely recognized, leaving much more research to be done. Statistically, most individuals with Asperger's will not make their living as mathematicians or produce Nobel Prize–winning scientific research even if talent is ingrained. Most individuals are going to have to make their way in the real world where they must coexist and diffuse problems as they surface. Therefore, more studies are needed that recognize our abilities to make outstanding employees who are conscientious and punctual. Until massive funding is devoted toward these sociological pursuits, it is up to us to make a name for ourselves and build a new type of stereotype for our peers.

That's right—it is up to us to use our positive Asperger's traits to bring enlightenment to parents and struggling individuals. The need for optimism and positive role models can be a powerful motivator. Identify your strengths, be courageous in honing them, and share what you have learned with others. This is how we can change the stereotypes and fears about Asperger's—by replacing them with the bold new reality we have created.

EPILOGUE

Your experience can teach others:
"Don't feel shackled and confined.
Just communicate directly to get out of a bind."

No insults are necessary, just the plain truth.
Bow out gracefully; never be uncouth.

Treat others with respect; expect the same in return.
With every negative experience, there is something each
    can learn.

Mutual respect must exist; healthy relationships feel good.
A friend has compassion; now that is understood.

Whenever you feel weak, recall what you've accomplished.
Think of the gloom you so valiantly abolished.

When your impulse is strong to return to your old ways.
Do something productive and look to brighter days.

Believe in yourself, and the decisions that you make.
Don't change your path; there is too much at stake.

You're stronger than you think, both now and tomorrow.
You truly have the power to eradicate deep sorrow.

Peace has now come, at the end of a long road.
You have been freed of the weight of a mighty load.

—Deborah Velazquez

Like many of you, I grew up on the Muppets from *Sesame Street* and the illusion they created. These inanimate pieces of fabric were given sentience and animation by Muppeteers crouching a few inches below the camera. With their funny voices and other characteristics, they may have made us proud to be a little silly and ridiculous. There was nothing normal about them, which was the whole point.

Someday *Sesame Street* should introduce a Muppet who is on the autism spectrum. His name should be Albert Newton (a composite of Albert Einstein and Isaac Newton, who are both rumored to have been on the autism spectrum). Albert is only eight years old but insists on dressing in gaudy suits with an untamed nest of blond hair and thick-rimmed glasses. His voice is loud and grating as though constantly shouting over multiple conversations. The Muppets of *Sesame Street* are a motley crew of gentle monsters and others are bizarre colors with noses as bulbous as lightbulbs. But Albert stands as a lone species. He is technically not bullied by the others, but nobody knows how to deal with his uniqueness. The other child Muppets are playing a board game, and Albert is ignored despite several attempts to join in the group activity.

Not now, Albert! Go play somewhere else for a little while.

Albert gives up and sits alone in the corner playing with a toy train. They mutter something about Albert being too strange to play in their group as a Muppet named Ginger is showing off a doll she received as a birthday present. After the group disperses, he notices that Ginger has left her doll behind.

The next scene shows a distraught Ginger pacing around her house wondering what has happened to her precious doll. Suddenly, there is a knock on the door, and it is Albert holding her lost birthday present. Ginger bursts into invisible tears of relief (because Muppets do not have tear ducts). When asked why he walked two miles throughout all of Sesame Street to return the doll, Albert replies without missing a beat:

Because I like you and thought you would be upset! I like collecting train models and would want someone to give them back if I left them behind.

Albert's act wins the permanent respect of Ginger, which trickles down to the rest of the child Muppets. They accept the strange suits and occasional outbursts. More important, their empathy toward Albert turns precocious as they develop the soft skills to redirect their new friend whenever he has been testing everyone's patience by talking about trains for a little too long. (He learns my personal rule of Five to Five—for every five minutes you spend talking about your interests, give others a chance to discuss their passions.) Most important, Albert learns to take an interest in the passions of his neurotypical friends while they give his interests a chance. One day, Albert has the courage to educate his new friends about Asperger's syndrome:

I have something called Asperger's, which is my superpower. It means I have trouble doing certain things like talking to new people and some noises really scare me. But there is so much that I am really good at, too. I can spell big words and do hard math problems.

As the friendship continues despite the occasional disagreement, it becomes clear they have more in common than initially believed.

Just like Albert Newton, it's time for us to build a new

identity that is separate from the clinical definitions grouping some of us together, one that is based on our gifts, not our deficiencies and challenges.

■ **Continue to be honest and a person of one's word.** This does not refer to the acidic, hurtful honesty that has created grief in the past. Rather, I am referring to the honesty that compels our population to return lost wallets, class rings, and other valuables. Your word is your iron bond, and integrity will pave the way for other opportunities.

■ **Remember that your growth will be accelerated by new experiences.** If you are not screwing up once in a while, then you are not trying as hard as you could. It would be a tremendous disservice to not open yourself to new experiences that are likely to conjure up social discomfort and even failure. The learning process is built by the bricks of failure and maturity must be earned.

■ **Hold on to what gives you happiness.** Even if it is ridiculous . . . it is important to be wise about what you choose to let go of as you push forward. If something gives us happiness and does not hurt or inconvenience others, then it is necessary to grasp it firmly. Plenty of us still hoard some toys and other Trinkets of Silliness. If you are calmed by the sensation of fondling magnetic beads in your pocket, then continue to use that as a calming mechanism for the future.

■ **Forgive yourself for past transgressions and look at yourself in the mirror.** In most of my speeches, I perform an exercise with members of the audience in which I hold up a purple handheld mirror purchased from CVS. The first mirror was always broken because it plummeted to the sidewalk one day as I was getting out of the car. It served as a metaphor because when we look at ourselves, we cannot help seeing the flaws that have become our legacy from years of unresolved misunderstandings and lack of closure. The days of childish stickers and other accolades for tiny accomplishments are fading memories. It is time to grow up and not be at the total mercy of others for your sense of worth. Know that you have a right to look inward once in a while to give to yourself what does not always come from someone else.

■ **Connect with your peers.** Some people may look at us and assume there is not a fragment of empathy. We are even accused of making people uncomfortable on purpose. In fact, we have tremendous empathy, and this incorrect assumption comes from sometimes failing to see the other person's point of view. Partnering with others in the autism community will help you on your journey. Sometimes it will feel like watching old video footage of yourself. It was occasionally hard for me to spend time with my peers when some of them made relentless phone calls or posted nonsensical, sometimes offensive content on my public Facebook wall. It was unbearable not because of the annoyance. It was the first time I had to witness many of my own behaviors and achieve the motivation to change.

■ **Accept advice and constructive criticism from those who genuinely care.** We will always live with the scars to some extent. We are haunted by the people who accused us of being ugly, stupid, weird, creepy, and other slurs that failed to motivate positive change. Regardless of how intense the individual effort may be, we cannot do everything ourselves and should embrace those in the neurotypical and autism community who can help us.

■ **Serve as the Catcher in the Rye for your younger peers.** *Catcher in the Rye* made J. D. Salinger a reluctant literary celebrity with his creation of the troubled Holden Caulfield. It was Holden's mission to block a cliff and save young children who are playing too close. While we cannot save all of our young peers from making mistakes and learning lessons the hardest way possible, perhaps we can at least try to provide some resources and support. Perhaps you are not able to let go. If this is the case, then pay it forward. One of the motivators for building your life is to become a role model for others in the throes of Asperger's syndrome who will benefit from your support.

■ **Have a sense of humor.** Humor is the nectar that we must squeeze out of our profound anguish. Do your best to chuckle at the occasional misunderstandings even though it may be hard to see past your bitterness in the moment. I think back to the day a woman nearly slapped me while trying to educate her about autism at a business luncheon. As she was telling me about a book that sounded familiar, I interjected: "Yes! *Look Me in the Eye!*"

The woman recoiled as though I had absentmindedly stared at her cleavage. It took five minutes to understand that she thought I had been ordering her to make eye contact when I was actually telling her the name of a popular book by John Elder Robison.

As you continue on your path to fulfilling adult life, the greatest gift you can give the world is to show society that our symptoms and assortment of eccentricities deserve another look. The obsessive persistence that people used to beat out of us with a verbal switch will be responsible for unusual accomplishments. As we push forward, the definition of Asperger's will begin to change, becoming synonymous with abilities and positive character traits as opposed to a defect needing correction.

I encourage you to embrace your Asperger's as well as some of the qualities that have been misunderstood and solicited rejections. True progress will come from knowing when to be silly, perseverate, act weird, and educate others about our condition. As you make progress, you will see the transformation of these so-called weaknesses into strengths. Having this "disability" will come to mean possessing abilities beyond your wildest dreams—abilities that will help you thrive as a successful adult. Successful, that is, by both Asperger's and neurotypical standards.

ACKNOWLEDGMENTS

First and foremost, my deepest gratitude goes out to my awesome editor, Marian Lizzi, and her assistant, Lauren Becker. Much appreciation is also extended to my longtime literary agents, Jeff Herman and Deborah Levine Herman.

My publicity team has been responsible for much of my success. They include Victor Gulotta from Gulotta Communications Inc., Melissa Broder from Penguin Group, Daphne Plump from D. Plump Consulting, and Michael Gaylin from Aurora Video.

A lion's share of credit is delegated to my family, especially my parents, Lewis and Janis Saperstein, who have uplifted me with a cocktail of pride, self-esteem, confidence, ambition, neuroticism, and prodding. The guilt and neuroses that will haunt my dreams forever are also responsible for creating the self-help tactic of "Reverse Procrastination." My sister, Dena S. Saperstein, has continued to embrace my Asperger's-ish points of view, and I will hopefully return the favor by looking at things from her perspective. Furthermore, my maternal grandmother, Brina Colby, has always supported me at every juncture of my journey.

I am extremely appreciative to the unsung heroes who took a chance on me and prevented me from becoming an unemployment statistic. My saviors include Neil Pollack, Cindy Mowris, Ray Germann, and Anthony Battista from Anderson Center for Autism (ACA); Michele Lawrenson; and Fred Erlich from Living Resources Inc. I am also incredibly proud of my talented creative writing students at Living Resources Inc.

Some professional colleagues include Kammy Kramer from the Minneapolis Chapter of Autism Speaks; Gwenn Canfield from ACCES-VR, Pete Colaizzo from the *Poughkeepsie Journal*, Amy Della Rocco and Joseph Dopico from Rehabilitation Support Services (RSS), Michael Buchanan and Diane Lang from Tin Roof Films, and Kelly Nye Lengerman from the University of Minnesota's LEND program. New York University worked with me during the "Keeping It Real" project (projectkeepitreal.com). I acknowledge Dr. Kristie Koenig, Aaron Lanou, Lauren Hough, Shravan Vidyarthi, and my fellow self-advocates, Dr. Stephen Shore and Zosia Zaks.

I would like to acknowledge my mentor, Stacey Orzell, who works with the Autism Move-a-Thon of Orange County (AMOC) and is the mother of young Eric, the New York State poster boy for autism. There is also Eric's older brother, Jason, and his father, Brian. A special thanks goes to Karen Kosack and Ellen M. Cordaro from the Hudson Valley Autism Society. I honor Anne Klingner from the Mental Health Association in Orange County Inc. and the Claudio Cares Foundation run by Luigi Coppola and Lisa Bajcar Coppola.

Thank you to John Kieran and the rest of the staff from the Blue Sky Ranch in Gardiner, New York, for getting me back safely on the ground after my first skydiving jump in August 2011. Furthermore, I appreciate all the community members who came out to support my efforts during the filming of *Free-Falling to End Bullying* (youtube.com/jessesaperstein) and the Anderson Foundation for Autism (AFA) who sponsored this adventure.

Personal accolades are extended to the Global and Regional Asperger Syndrome Partnership (GRASP) and its leaders, Michael John Carley, Kate Palmer, Karl Wittig, and Steve Katz, and all of the group members.

Standing by me are my loyal friends, Karl A. Brautigam III, Emilie Britton, Chris Courchaine, Richard Carroll, Charles Perez, Andy and Vivian Rose, Lisa Odendahl, Mark Schneider, Mateo Prendergast, Ray and Trudy Zarcone, Brian Liston, Samantha Michaels, Jason Cohen, Ruby Randig, Jocelynn Banfield, Jay and Maura Liguori, Cari Allen, Dario Malcolm, Tina Bruton-Rimpinen, Josephine Bila, Deborah Velazquez, Dr. Michael Caldwell, Jim Hanlon, Shannon Lashlee, Lora Gilmore, and Jennifer Maples-Obrizok.

Educators in the Arlington Central School District and at Hobart and William Smith Colleges have touched my life. Special recognition goes out to the president of Hobart and William Smith Colleges, Mark Gearan; his wife, Mary Gearan; as well as their daughters, Madeleine and Kathleen.

I have been blessed by the incredible community of Dutchess County, New York, and the surrounding areas who continue to nurture my growth well into adulthood. I would also like to acknowledge Marcus Molinaro who is the Dutchess County executive and is raising a beautiful daughter with autism named Abigail.

My younger peers continue to remind me that they have something incredible to offer. They are Nick Scott, Todd Weaver, Elliot Kramer, Joshua Adams, Tyler Talbot, Nathaniel Sherwood, Brett

Alan Hale, Chris Odendahl, Sam Andrews, Aiden Zarcone, Brendan Caldwell, Casey Kosack, Alexis Kosack, Kyle Lombardi, Madeline Allen, and Sean Hammond.

Finally, I owe everything to Joey and Carol DiPaolo as well as the courageous campers of Camp Teens Living a Challenge (TLC). You were with me when I took my first steps on the Appalachian Trail and were the catalyst for everything that followed.

RESOURCES

ORGANIZATIONS

The Global and Regional Asperger Syndrome Partnership (GRASP)

grasp.org

GRASP has been a pioneer since 2003 when the organization was formed. It was founded by Michael John Carley, author of *Asperger's from the Inside Out,* and a widely respected advocate. The novelty of GRASP is that it runs on the gears of those who actually have Asperger's syndrome because we comprise some of the most powerful advocates. GRASP is known for its network of support groups that meet an average of once a month in New York, Los Angeles, Philadelphia, Tennessee, and other major U.S. cities. The gatherings always revolve around a specific topic pertaining to adulthood, such as employment, dating, and anger management. Even though meeting times are limited to once a month, the group usually branches out into social outings, such as museum visits that are periodically announced on the Facebook page.

If a group does not exist in your area, you can contact GRASP and create your own.

GRASP
419 Lafayette Street
New York, NY 10003
(888) 474-7277 (888-47-GRASP)
info@grasp.org

Wrong Planet
wrongplanet.net

Our community's version of Facebook exists on this popular website for youths and adults on the autism spectrum. It was launched in 2004 by Alex Plank, who is a self-advocate diagnosed at the age of nine and who currently serves as a consultant to the lead actress and creators of the FX series *The Bridge*. There are guest blog posts related to common issues, such as stressors during the holiday season, romantic endeavors, and more obscure topics, such as losing one's wallet. There is also the option of posting chat topics on a public forum and receiving advice from an army of individuals with the personal experience of being on the spectrum themselves. While professionals are invaluable toward our success, the most profound advice will come from one of our peers. There is also a chat room and media section.

The National Autistic Society
autism.org.uk

This organization is based out of the United Kingdom but has some invaluable information on how to help us thrive in the world.

It is a cornucopia of resources with topics like "All About Diagnosis," "Understanding Behavior," "Benefits and Community Care," and "Strategies and Approaches." Unlike other websites, the focus is on finding resources in adulthood. Something that is most unique about this site is the section that acknowledges how individuals with autism are often the target of legal misunderstandings and offers resources on how to advocate for those individuals who are embroiled in the legal system. You will also find real-life stories from people who have autism, neurotypical romantic partners of those on the autism spectrum, stories from siblings, and tales from parents and caregivers.

The National Autistic Society
393 City Road
London EC1V 1NG
United Kingdom
44 (0)20 7833 2299
nas@nas.org.uk

Asperger's Association of New England (AANE)
aane.org

AANE is a vast library of resources that was founded in 1996 by a group of parents and professionals who were concerned about the future of those with autism after Asperger's syndrome was recognized as a disability in the DSM-IV. Their mission is to provide education and referrals to individuals with Asperger's, their family members, and professionals trying to help them reach their potential. People often perform their greatest work when they have a personal connection to the issue and most (if not all) of the staff have had experience with Asperger's with their children, siblings, and close friends. The organization also employs individuals with Asperger's syndrome. What is most admirable about this organization is that it is not necessary to have an actual diagnosis of Asperger's to receive services. Their help also expands to other neurological differences or those experiencing the same struggles as those on the autism spectrum.

Asperger's Association of New England (AANE)
51 Water Street, Suite 206
Watertown, MA 02472
(617) 393-3824
info@aane.org

College and University Support Programs (CUSP)
cuspservices.com

CUSP is one of the rare resources entirely devoted to preparing students with Asperger's syndrome for the often difficult transition to college life. The program deals with deficiencies related to executive functioning skills, self-advocacy, organization, structuring an abundance of free time, and the typical attitudes that can spoil one's college experience. This support extends beyond the transition from high school to college as services are geared toward preparing students beyond graduation by honing their skills as a valuable employee for any business. As their leader Stephen Motto says, "Failures should be seen as teachers and not an opportunity to feel bad about oneself."

College and University Support Programs (CUSP)
P.O. Box 66367
Albany, NY 12206
(518) 203-3913
info@cuspservices.com
admissions@cuspservices.com

The Daniel Jordan Fiddle Foundation for Adult Autism

djfiddlefoundation.org

The Daniel Jordan Fiddle Foundation was founded in 2002 by Linda Walder Fiddle in memory of her son, Danny, who was affected by an autism spectrum disorder. Aside from providing an abundance of resources, the foundation revolves around providing grants specifically geared toward the lives of young people making the transition into adult life and the innovative projects they are launching. Past grant awards have focused on educating the public about adults living with an ASD. One of the initiatives they have pioneered is a three-year project that began in 2011 with the Autistic Self-Advocacy Network (ASAN). It is known as the Empowering Autistic Leaders Manual and includes articles written by adults on the spectrum. It also provides guidance and problem-solving initiatives as people advocate for themselves within college programs. They have also pioneered the first support group catered for individuals at least fifty years of age to focus on issues related to health, aging, and new innovations in the world of ASD. This group meets once a month and is run by a facilitator from the Global and Regional Asperger Syndrome Partnership (GRASP). There are also recreational programs run out of the Ridgewood, New Jersey YMCA that allow families to experience Danny's Red Ball Weekends and embrace the magic of an ASD.

The Daniel Jordan Fiddle Foundation
P.O. Box 1149
Ridgewood, NJ 07451
info@djfiddlefoundation.org

BOOKS

Look Me in the Eye: My Life with Asperger's
John Elder Robison (Crown, 2007)

Look Me in the Eye is about the adventures of John Elder Robison who used his Asperger's savant abilities to design fire-breathing and rocket-launching guitars for the band KISS during the 1970s. He is the younger brother of memoirist Augusten Burroughs who is best known for his book *Running with Scissors*, which was adapted into a feature film.

John came of age during a time when Asperger's was judged as a character flaw as opposed to an actual condition. His suffering was augmented by an alcoholic father and a mentally ill mother. Not to mention dropping out of high school in the tenth grade. This book is a great read due to its humor as John's childhood was filled with over-the-top pranks. He accepted his quirks, which were ultimately responsible for great innovations that extended to developments at the toy company Milton Bradley. The greatest lesson taught by *Look Me in the Eye* is that not everybody is going to accept your uniqueness, but a few reasonable compromises will make a huge difference over the long term.

Mozart and the Whale: An Asperger's Love Story
Jerry and Mary Newport with Johnny Dodd (Touchstone, 2007)

Mozart and the Whale is probably one of the most bizarre, but beautiful, love stories ever written. Unlike the fictional film *Adam*, it is a nonfiction story about how romance can bloom between two very different people with Asperger's syndrome. Jerry Newport is a mathematical savant with limited social graces, an obsession with birds, and an endless résumé of different jobs. Mary Meinel is an artistically inclined woman with a traumatic childhood who has been committed to mental hospitals as an adult. But her spacey demeanor made her the perfect choice to play a Bolian character on *Star Trek: Deep Space Nine* in the 1990s. The lives of Jerry and Mary touch upon common issues that plague the autism community. These issues include persistence that is seen as borderline stalking, hoarding, Internet addiction, employment struggles, and sexual assault of women on the spectrum. Sexual assault of women on the autism spectrum is far more common than people realize, and it is a testament to their hidden struggles.

Mozart and the Whale earned its title because Jerry chose to dress up as a whale and Mary was Wolfgang Mozart for a costume party. On that note, the book emphasizes the importance of support groups and organized activities catered to those who are on the spectrum. *Mozart and the Whale* has also been adapted into a feature film starring Josh Hartnett and Radha Mitchell as the main characters.

Asperger's from the Inside Out: A Supportive and Practical Guide for Anyone with Asperger's Syndrome
Michael John Carley (Perigee, 2008)

Michael John Carley is the founder and former executive director of the Global and Regional Asperger Syndrome Partnership (GRASP). Like John Elder Robison, Michael lived most of his life without a diagnosis, but found some answers after his son was diagnosed. *Asperger's from the Inside Out* provides guidance for adults living on the autism spectrum who are struggling with issues related to disclosure, finding coping strategies, and procuring employment that caters to at least some of their strengths. There is also a chapter devoted to helping individuals move forward despite their memories of consistent bullying throughout childhood.

Much of the book is autobiographical and anecdotal. It takes us back to a time when we were undiagnosed and our uniqueness may have been perceived as a character flaw or disruption. With that said, it is time to look back on those years and forgive ourselves for such behaviors that were misunderstood by teachers and family.

Different . . . Not Less: Inspiring Stories of Achievement and Successful Employment from Adults with Autism, Asperger's, and ADHD
Temple Grandin and Tony Attwood (Future Horizons, 2012)

Dr. Temple Grandin and Tony Attwood provide a collection of real-life stories from fourteen adults on the autism spectrum who have found success in the world of employment. These adults thrive in different fields, such as medicine, art, technology, and sales throughout various Western cultures. Some have even emerged from incarceration and a history of alcohol abuse. These contributors did not learn about their Asperger's until they were well into adulthood and were thus deprived of many resources that the younger generation enjoys today starting in early childhood. *Different . . . Not Less* has been praised for the diversity of its contributors, which argues against the stereotype that most individuals with Asperger's are socially awkward geniuses.

Different Like Me: My Book of Autism Heroes
Jennifer Elder and Marc Thomas (Jessica Kingsley, 2005)

While this picture book is technically meant for children, it will offer comfort well into adulthood. Profiled is a long roster of cultural icons and all of whom (except Dr. Temple Grandin) have been posthumously diagnosed with Asperger's syndrome. Their uniqueness may not have been readily embraced by society, but these differences led to fame and even fortune. Some highlights of *Different Like Me* include descriptions about Hans Christian Andersen (Danish author of *The Little Mermaid*) who was born on April 2 (Autism Awareness

Day) and Charles Lutwidge Dodgson (aka Lewis Carroll) who was the Oxford mathematician turned nonsensical children's storyteller of the *Alice's Adventures in Wonderland* books.

Pretending to Be Normal: Living with Asperger's Syndrome
Liane Holliday Willey (Jessica Kingsley, 1999)

Liane Holliday Willey is a beautiful woman with three gorgeous young daughters. When one of her twins was diagnosed with Asperger's syndrome, Liane realized she was also on the autism spectrum and finally found answers. Her story accurately describes the plight of women with Asperger's syndrome who are often underrepresented in the autism community because the condition affects men four times more often. Liane describes strategies that have allowed her to adapt to the neurotypical world and raise a beautiful family. While much of the book is autobiographical and filled with colorful anecdotes, *Pretending to Be Normal* is also a self-help book filled with tips on organization, reducing stress, and confronting sensory overload (especially if someone does not like being touched), and the sensitive topic of disclosing to loved ones. Unlike other resources that focus on the deficiencies chained to Asperger's, Liane emphasizes the strengths and how small modifications or compromises may lead to success. The greatest gift of her book is the way it challenges readers to redefine their perception of the word "normal." *Pretending to Be Normal* also had a cameo in the 2009 feature film *Adam*.

ABOUT THE AUTHOR

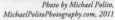

Photo by Michael Polito,
MichaelPolitoPhotography.com, 2011

Jesse A. Saperstein was diagnosed with a form of autism called Asperger's syndrome (AS) in 1996 at age fourteen. After graduating from Hobart and William Smith Colleges in 2004 with a bachelor's degree in English, Jesse completed the 2,174-mile Appalachian Trail to benefit the Joey DiPaolo AIDS Foundation, raising more than $19,000 for Camp TLC (Teens Living a Challenge).

Jesse's memoir, *Atypical: Life with Asperger's in 20⅓ Chapters* was published by Perigee Books in April 2010. His story's practical advice and outrageous humor placed Jesse as a media personality, motivational speaker, and most important, an advocate for people with disabilities.

After receiving a grant from the Anderson Foundation for Autism (AFA) in Staatsburg, New York, Jesse completed his first skydiving jump, filmed in *Free-Falling to End Bullying*, to help eradicate bullying (youtube.com/jessesaperstein). He was also one of three prominent autism advocates working with New York University to design an anti-bullying curriculum for New York City public schools with the "Keeping It Real Project" (projectkeepitreal.com). He has pioneered and currently teaches a creative writing curriculum for Living Resources Inc. in Albany, New York, for individuals with disabilities.

Jesse visits schools and organizations, where he has been successful in wiping out bullying or at least dramatically alleviating it with every presentation. His next goals are to hike the 2,600-mile Pacific Crest Trail and introduce the first Muppet with autism to *Sesame Street*.

Jesse currently lives in Pleasant Valley, New York, with his family. He may be reached at JesseASaperstein@gmail.com. His websites are jessesaperstein.com and youtube.com/jessesaperstein.

Photo by James "Big Jim" Cupples and Skydive the Ranch, copyright © August 2011